# TAKE CONTROL OF YOUR LIFE

*Overcoming Life's Obstacles,
Difficult Emotions
and Problem Behavior*

Brad Garrett

ISBN 978-1-956010-75-6 (paperback)
ISBN 978-1-956010-76-3 (hardcover)
ISBN 978-1-956010-77-0 (digital)

Copyright © 2021 by Brad Garrett

All rights reserved. No part of this publication may be reproduced, distributed, or transmitted in any form or by any means, including photocopying, recording, or other electronic or mechanical methods without the prior written permission of the publisher. For permission requests, solicit the publisher via the address below.

Rushmore Press LLC
1 800 460 9188
www.rushmorepress.com

Printed in the United States of America

# TABLE OF CONTENTS

Introduction . . . . . . . . . . . . . . . . . . . . . . . . . . . . . . . . . v

1. What Do You Think About Emotions? . . . . . . . . . . . . . . . . 1
2. Where Do Emotions Begin?. . . . . . . . . . . . . . . . . . . . . . . 7
3. Emotions Have to Be Shut Off . . . . . . . . . . . . . . . . . . . . 16
4. The Consequences of Not Controlling Your Emotions . . . . 26
5. A Biblical Perspective on Emotions . . . . . . . . . . . . . . . . . 36
6. Controlling the Acute Stress Response . . . . . . . . . . . . . . . 45
7. Controlling the Immediate Behavioral Response . . . . . . . . 54
8. The Golden Key to Change . . . . . . . . . . . . . . . . . . . . . . 62
9. What Makes Up Our Thinking . . . . . . . . . . . . . . . . . . . 72
10. A Biblical Perspective on Thinking. . . . . . . . . . . . . . . . . 87
11. Thinking and Who We Are . . . . . . . . . . . . . . . . . . . . . 94
12. A Biblical Perspective on a Man's Heart . . . . . . . . . . . . . 102
13. Thinking Strategies . . . . . . . . . . . . . . . . . . . . . . . . . . . 111
14. Difficult Emotions. . . . . . . . . . . . . . . . . . . . . . . . . . . . 120
15. Problem Behavior . . . . . . . . . . . . . . . . . . . . . . . . . . . 133
16. Reprogram Your Brain. . . . . . . . . . . . . . . . . . . . . . . . 151
17. A Biblical Perspective: Spiritual Harmony . . . . . . . . . . . 160
18. Low-Energy Negative Emotions. . . . . . . . . . . . . . . . . . 178
19. Stress 101: The Basics . . . . . . . . . . . . . . . . . . . . . . . . 190
20. Tips for Improving Your Life . . . . . . . . . . . . . . . . . . . 199
21. What Have You Learned?. . . . . . . . . . . . . . . . . . . . . . 209

Notes . . . . . . . . . . . . . . . . . . . . . . . . . . . . . . . . . . . . . . 217

# INTRODUCTION

Picture a nice friendly neighborhood on a late Saturday afternoon. Neighbors are working in their yards and garages, washing cars, and starting up barbecues. Children are playing outside in their yards and the older boys are playing ball in the street. Music plays from an ice cream vendor's truck down the street. Location: Anytown, USA.

A familiar voice breaks the silence, "This is Maple Street in the last calm and reflective moments before the monsters came out."

"The Monsters Are Due on Maple Street" is a 1960 Twilight Zone episode that provides an insightful look into human behavior under unusual circumstances.

Unfortunately, the people in the television story do not rise to the occasion to become heroes; instead, they fell prey to their negative emotions and behaviors.

As the scene progresses, the neighborhood skies quickly darken temporarily as something passes overhead. What was it? A meteor, a spaceship?

Someone shouts out that they have no electrical power. Another says the phone lines are down, and as someone attempts to drive for help, they find all the car batteries are dead.

Then a young boy speaks up, "They don't want us to leave!"

Who are they?

Fear starts to creep in, and their thinking is becoming irrational.

Hours earlier, they were neighbors, friends, but fear changes this. They become suspicious of one another. It begins with the neighbor across the street who acts differently from them. Surely, they must be one of them. *Rational, calm,* and *reflective thought* have left the building.

The neighbors progress to turning on the only rational person left who is trying to prevent them from attacking the neighbor. Soon, their suspicions expand to include each other.

Their fears and anxieties drive their irrational behavior. They grow more aggressive, and then violent. The monsters have come out on Maple Street.

In our own Twilight Zone episode, it starts on a beautiful spring day in March 2020, then COVID-19 happened; lockdowns began, jobs were lost, and schools were closed. Mental health problems increased, and suicide rates rose, especially among teens. The fear, anxiety, and anger began driving people's behavior as the monsters came out in America in 2020.

The people on Maple Street are ordinary people, like you and me, who go through an unusual experience. An important point in this story is how people's fears take over, altering their thinking and behavior. When rational thought is lost and negative emotions take control, people change, and the monster comes out.

As a marriage and family therapist, I see the monster that can come out when people no longer control their emotions, allowing bad behavior to hurt others. I have seen the monster in criminal behavior, substance abuse, and a selfish, self-centered lifestyle. The monster hides in the shadows.

I conducted numerous anger and stress management groups as well as corrective thinking classes and supervised domestic violence groups. I worked with delinquent youth who had difficulty controlling their emotions, had mental health issues, and had committed violent crimes.

Working together with these delinquent adolescents, and the men and women who were in DV groups, I watched as they made the changes in their life to achieve successful and productive lives. What did they need to do? They needed to learn how to have control over their emotions, behavior, and negative thinking.

Shortly before leaving juvenile court, I put together a police officers' standard training program entitled "Manage Your Emotions: Manage Your Life" for the two hundred fifty juvenile probation officers I worked with. The purpose of the training was to educate them on the negative impact emotions like stress, anger, and anxiety can have on their physical and mental health. It also included how to take control over those emotions and maintain a healthy mental and emotional lifestyle at work and home.

This book is educational. Its true purpose, though, is to be applicational. It is similar to the Dummies series in providing education about emotions, behavior, and thinking, followed by how to apply what you have read. The information I share in this book has helped many adolescents and adults improve their lives and overcome things that they previously struggled with.

If you are looking for a book on improving your mental, emotional, and physical health going forward, this one is for you.

Information by itself will change nothing for you. When information leads to understanding, understanding will lead to application, and when application is combined with effort, everything can change.

What is it that you would like to change in 2021 and beyond?

# What Do You Think About Emotions?

*"May I say that I have not thoroughly
enjoyed serving with humans,
I find their illogic and foolish emotions a constant irritant."*
-Spock

We live in a fast-paced world today—that is, unless you are fortunate enough to live in the countryside like my oldest son and his family. Life there tends to be a bit slower, but even those folks have their share of problems. The demands of life—personal, family, and work—cry out for constant attention. Which need do I meet first? Which ones will need to be put off? As humans, we cannot meet all the demands that are constantly made on us. This can lead to feeling stressed out and overwhelmed. There never seems to be any time for relaxing. If you are a single parent, finding time for yourself is near to impossible! But it needs to happen.

Many people are dog-paddling through life, trying to keep their heads above water before the next wave comes crashing in. There were a lot of waves in 2020. A lot of people are simply surviving life; they are not really enjoying life. The continual demands, coupled with large amounts of financial debt, can suck the joy out of your life like a vampire draining your blood. Many people I talk with feel exhausted at the end of their day. Then they have to get up tomorrow and do it all over again. No wonder life can feel out of control at times. If any of this sounds familiar, then you have come to the right place for help.

America saw a rise in mental health issues in both adults and adolescents in 2020. Many people are struggling today emotionally, while others may have recently experienced mental health issues due to the pressures they are under. Suicides went up among struggling teens due to the closure of schools. Isolation further exacerbates mental health issues.

Good mental health is closely connected to good emotional health, called emotional regulation, which means good emotional control. A large percentage of the delinquent adolescents I worked with struggled to control their emotions on a daily basis even without a mental health diagnosis. And what I see today is that the adults are experiencing the same problems.

## What Do You Think?

It is important for you to explore what you think about emotions. What comes to mind? Is your first thought about an emotion you struggle with, a positive emotion that causes you to feel good, or a negative one that has the opposite effect? Do you think about the bad behavior that occurs when you lose control? Do you believe that controlling your negative emotions is possible?

Most people do not give emotions a second thought until their emotions get out of control. We do not spend time thinking about why we emotionally react.

Life's demands and the time pressure that comes with them can cause you to feel like life is spinning out of control. The more demands that are made on you, the more internal pressure you feel. The more pressure you feel, the more emotionally reactive you become. A friend of mine recently apologized for being a little short (emotionally reactive) with me over the phone, explaining she was having a stressful morning when I called.

If you could take control over any emotion today, what emotion would it be? What problem behavior would you like to overcome and change? What bad habits do you want to break? As we begin, it would be a good thing for you to identify what you would like to change about yourself.

# Emotions

What is the purpose of emotion? The first seems to be obvious; emotions add color to our lives and spice things up. If colors were limited to black and white, things would become boring, and if food had no spice to flavor it, food would become bland. In like manner, life without emotions would be boring and bland.

Who would want to go through life without experiencing love or not feel the thrill that comes when your team scores the winning touchdown? But emotions have a dark side, like the hurt you feel when a relationship ends or the disappointment that comes when your promotion is denied.

It is impossible to have only one set of emotions (the positive ones) without the reality of a second set of emotions (the negative ones). We love the positive emotions but are not too happy with the negative ones, especially when we see them in someone else. Oh, but not us! Positive and negative emotions are a fact of life. Emotions shake things up, keep life interesting, and contribute to being human.

Are emotions good or bad? They are neither good nor bad; they are simply a feeling that is produced by an outside stimulus that causes you to react. We have given emotions names to define them so that we can distinguish one emotion from another, be able to identify what we are feeling, and then communicate what we are feeling to others.

The good or bad of emotion is related to how we behave once we feel it. Anger, for instance, is an emotion that can lead to bad behavior by hitting someone. This can lead to being arrested and placed into an anger management or domestic violence group. A person does not get arrested for being angry. They are arrested for the bad behavior they did when they were angry.

It is important to understand as we begin that every emotion translates into some type of behavior that expresses that emotion. When a person is in love, they do things that show they are in love, like buying flowers. When a person is angry, they may do things like yell, cuss, and name-call. How a person behaves when they experience an emotion communicates what they are feeling.

## Emotions Teach Us About Ourselves

Emotions can teach us about ourselves if we pay attention. Learning about yourself is key in learning how to control your emotions and change your behavior. Understanding why you react in certain ways in specific situations is important in learning how to control your emotions in future situations.

Everyone experiences emotions like stress and anger, but not everyone experiences those emotions in the same way. If ten people attend the same football game, will these ten people react emotionally in the same way during the game? Not a chance!

Although everyone is experiencing the same event, their reactions will differ based on each one's personal framework, who are they rooting for. When the game is over, one person will be happy because their team won, while another may feel disappointed that their team lost. Same event, different emotional outcome.

People do not experience the same emotion in the same way as others may. For one, the level of intensity of that emotion will differ between people. One person may become very vocal about their team, while another sits quietly rooting for theirs.

Learning how to control your emotions begins with personal awareness. To make changes you will need to slow down, separate yourself from the busyness of the day at times, and reflect on what is going on in you and around you. Insight will give you the answers to your struggles without having to go to a professional counselor. Insight looks beyond what happened, to what is happening in you right now.

Insight helps to take your past experiences, memories, and thinking, and apply how they contribute to what you are experiencing in the present moment.

## Psychological and Spiritual Perspective on Emotions

Throughout the book, we will look at emotions, behavior, and thinking from a psychological perspective, and at times, a spiritual one. Psychology is loosely defined as the study of the human mind, conscious and unconscious, and human behavior. We will look at the psychological principles behind thinking, emotional control, and behavior change.

Psychology helps to provide a basic framework for understanding human emotions and behavior. Emotions, behavior, and thinking, are intertwined in emotional reactions like three strands in a rope. The good news is that as you begin to work on making a change in any one of these three areas, it will automatically have a positive effect for change on the other two.

Psychology does not look at man as a spiritual being, it looks at man based on a humanistic point of view; meaning man is fully capable of solving all his own problems. He is not in need of something outside of himself to do this, which I believe is a blind spot. Psychology does not understand the significance of the spiritual and its connection to man's existence.

Therapeutic spirituality is loosely defined by how the client wants to define it. This approach tends to relate spirituality to higher thought, or greater consciousness and awareness. There are no concrete guiding principles in spirituality. The same is true with A.A., which defines spirituality as a higher power.

I will approach emotions, behavior, and thinking from a Christian perspective, using the Bible as my source. The Bible has a lot of insight into these three areas, and how to make the needed changes to experience a more calm, peaceful, and joyous lifestyle. The spiritual dimension can be a valuable asset to help you bring about the changes you want to make in your life.

# *Where Do Emotions Begin?*

> *"Anyone who has ever asked for directions knows you need two crucial pieces of information to get good results: a starting point and a destination."*
> -Mike Quigley

Many of you may have watched a documentary on Africa, or at least watched a scene in a movie where there is a lion chasing a zebra or gazelle. It usually begins near a watering hole where all the animals are gathering for a drink.

Most of the animals there are friendly toward one another; they are grazers. But up on a hill not too far away are the predators, the meat-eaters, the lions. The lions are watching the activity at the watering hole and picking out their meal for the day. Slowly they get up and start to make their way toward the intended prey. I have seen it happen in my yard as a cat starts to make its way slowly and quietly toward a bird it wants to catch. Suddenly the animal makes its break toward its intended target, and the bird flies off.

At the watering hole when the zebra senses it is in danger, it is off to the races. Who will win, the predator or the intended victim? Both animals are operating off the survival instinct called fight-or-flight. Their lives depend on how they respond. Fight-or-flight is an instinctive physiological response to a threatening situation that readies the animal to either resist the threat with force or run away.

Fight-or-flight results in a burst of energy that is needed for the zebra to run for its life. When the fight-or-flight response turns on, the zebra does not have to take the time to think if it should run; it runs.

We have all experienced fight-or-flight at some point in life. It may have been when someone jumped out from a hiding place and scared you, or when you went to a scary movie and jumped when the creature appeared on the screen. It can happen when you are concentrating on something and do not notice that someone has walked up behind you. When they spoke, it startled you.

## What Happens in Fight-or-Flight?

You may be asking yourself what fight-or-flight has to do with emotions. Good question. It is all tied to how the brain responds in certain situations. In fight-or-flight, the brain and autonomic nervous system work together to produce the desired action—run away or fight. There is also a freeze response that can be seen when a deer freezes in the headlights of a car at night. We will focus on the run or fight responses.

Fight-or-flight results in a physiological response in the body that is caused by a chemical release into the animal's bloodstream. These chemicals, called hormones, produce the energy needed to respond to a threat.

Fight-or-flight begins with sensory information called a stimulus. Sensory information is what the zebra hears, smells, or sees. The zebra's brain interprets the stimulus—in this case, the lion—as to whether it is a threat or not. Once the zebra interprets the stimulus, a decision is made on how to respond.

Sensory information is received by a part of the brain called the amygdala. The amygdala's primary role in fight-or-flight is to *process information from the stimulus* to determine whether it is a threat. In humans the amygdala works the same way, creating an emotion.

If the amygdala interprets the stimulus in a way that creates an emotional response, a message is sent to the hypothalamus, a separate area of the brain. The hypothalamus sends a message to the autonomic nervous system and the adrenal glands to activate. Stay with me on this because it has relevance to how emotional reactions work.

The adrenal glands release the hormones adrenaline and cortisol, which affect the operation of the sympathetic and parasympathetic nervous systems. The sympathetic system is like a green traffic light for go, and the parasympathetic system is a yellow or red light for slow down or stop.

The sympathetic nervous system speeds things up like the heart rate, which is caused when adrenaline is released in the bloodstream. This produces the physiological changes needed in fight-or-flight. These include:

- Heart rate, pulse, and blood pressure increase.
- Breathing becomes rapid.
- Increased blood flow.
- Release of blood sugar to supply the muscles with energy, speed, and strength.
- Increase in muscle tension.
- Heightened awareness.
- Pupils dilate.
- Focus narrows (similar to tunnel vision).

The adrenal glands pump out a second hormone called cortisol, the stress hormone. Cortisol works in the opposite way by slowing down parts of the parasympathetic nervous system. These changes include but are not limited to.

- Digestion slows.

- Elimination of bodily fluids is temporarily on hold.
- Tissue repair is put on hold.
- Inhibition of sexual arousal.
- Suppression of the immune system. We will talk more about this later.

Everything you just read regarding the physiological changes to your body from these two hormones happens within seconds.

In addition to processing the stimulus, the amygdala plays a role in *memory* and *decision-making*. Once the animal senses a threat, the amygdala, based on past experiences *(memory)*, knows how to respond in the present situation *(decision-making)*. Fight-or-flight is an efficient and necessary survival response in animals. The animal does not have to stop and think about what to do each time it senses a threat.

## And Then It Stops

Once the animal is out of danger the physiological changes stop, hormones dissipate, and the body returns to a pre-fight-or-flight level. Fight-or-flight continues only as long as the animal perceives a threat. All the bodily changes that take place in the zebra are for its survival, and when the animal is safe, the physiological changes reverse and the animal returns to a state of calm. At least until another threat is perceived.

Fight-or-flight works similar to a home security light system. Your home's security lights are programmed to turn on when something enters into a programmed area that the lights cover. When the lights turn on, it is similar to the amygdala reacting to a perceived threat. Emotions turn on in the very same way as the security lights do when something enters the programmed area they cover.

The security lights stay on as long as movement is detected. Once the object that turned the lights on moves out of the programmed range of coverage, the lights turn off. When the zebra is out of danger, fight-or-flight turns off. The home security system works in a similar way to fight-or-flight, they turn on when something enters the programmed area, and turn off when it is gone. Unfortunately, although emotions work on the same principle as fight-or-flight to turn on, emotions do not automatically turn off when the event that caused them is over.

## Emotions Are Energy

It may have seemed odd to start our discussion on emotions by talking about animals and fight-or-flight. What has fight-or-flight got to do with emotions? Pretty much everything. In humans, the fight-or-flight response is called the *acute stress response*. Emotions are the result of the amygdala's response to an external stimulus. For the zebra, it's the lion; in humans, it's someone calling you a name, being late for work, or not getting what you want.

When you react to an external stimulus such as being called a name, stuck in traffic and late for work, the acute stress response turns on the same way as in fight-or-flight. The amygdala determines if the stimulus is worth an emotional response. Negative emotions such as stress, anger, and anxiety are emotions that function in the same way as an animal fleeing for its life.

Emotional responses happen quickly. Anger is an immediate response to something that just happened to you or someone said to you. You were not angry prior to this, but now you are.

When you compare the list of physiological changes that take place in fight-or-flight to the physiological changes that come with high-energy negative emotions, there is no difference. Take a moment and review these changes in the last chapter. As you read each one, pause and see if you experience any of these physiological responses when you experience stress, anger, or anxiety.

## Emotional Energy

Emotions are energy felt in the body, similar to electrical energy that can be felt. Have you ever touched a live wire and received a shock? Electrical energy has the power to turn things on like a light. Electrical energy can be turned off too.

Emotional energy is turned on by the body's physiological response to a stimulus. What is important to know is that emotional energy can be turned off at any time.

Thinking of emotions as energy can quickly get you in touch with what is happening inside you. The energy you feel when you become angry is no different than the emotional energy created by stress, anxiousness, or irritation. The source of the energy in high-energy negative emotions is the same, the release of adrenaline.

Emotions create either positive or negative energy. As we progress, I want you to become familiar with the negative energy you feel every time you become angry, stressed, or anxious. Awareness of what is going on inside you is important if you want to change it.

Negative emotions can be broken into two categories, high or low energy. A type of high-energy emotion is anger while a low-energy emotion is depression. High-energy and low-energy emotions follow different pathways in the brain and body. They are also expressed in different types of behavior. As we start our focus will be on high-energy emotions. We will cover the low-energy emotions later.

Looking at negative emotions as energy felt in your body is meant to help you become more aware of what is happening inside you. When you stay focused on what happened to you instead of what is happening inside you, you fall into a trap that allows the emotion and energy to continue. Focusing on what happened will only prolong the amount of time it takes to get over it and recover from the emotion. Becoming aware of the negative energy is a much quicker way to identify what you are feeling and respond by shutting it down.

## Emotions and Health

A second reason to look at emotions as energy, especially negative energy, is to connect that energy to the damage emotions can have on your physical health. If you explore websites like Mayo Clinic or WebMD, you will find suggestions for how to improve your health regarding a variety of diseases such as high blood pressure and heart disease. One suggestion made over and over again is to lower your stress level.

I believe this suggestion applies to all high-energy negative emotions. These medical websites recommend activities to lower stress such as exercise, yoga, and meditation to name a few. It is important you take an active role in maximizing good health by learning how to control your emotions, especially stress.

The health problems that stress can create start now, but the results are not seen until years later. The damage to our bodies created by stress takes place in a similar way that damage is done to a football player's brain from repeated blows to the head. The damage that is being done in the present time does not show up until years later. The problems created in the present by ongoing stress may not show up until years later, but the damage is being done now.

One way to lower the risk of developing health-related problems in the future is to learn how to control your stress, anger, anxiety, and any other negative emotion that is affecting you.

The major focus on improving health problems is usually on medication first, followed by all the obvious things you need to do like exercise and eat healthy. Very little is said by doctors about getting your emotional life, mainly stress, under control. Once in a while, you might hear a person say that their doctor told them they need to take time to relax.

Understanding you have the ability to control your negative emotions, including stress, goes a long way in being able to turn around certain health issues. In addition, you should want to experience more positive emotions in your life daily life, which can be lost when the negative emotions take over.

## High-Energy Negative Emotions

Anger, anxiety, stress, and fear are the most common high-energy negative emotions. There are many other high-energy emotions such as frightened, threatened, worried, irritated, annoyed, frustrated, upset, touchy, agitated, irate, rage, and impatience. The list could go on, but all you need to recognize is that these high-energy emotions result from adrenaline. Too much adrenaline in your life is your enemy.

I was recently speaking to a young woman who works in law enforcement and had recently developed some health problems. I was sharing with her that in addition to the things she is doing with her doctor, she will need to learn how to deal with her negative emotions, especially stress, and turn off the adrenaline.

Many of the probation officers I worked with had difficulty turning their emotions off after leaving work, allowing the adrenaline to continue in their bodies for longer than they needed to.

This may be no different for you when leaving work. Do you have a problem turning the stress off? I have heard it said by many probation officers that the stress and adrenaline that comes with their work are always on.

Police, probation, and detention officers, based on the type of work they do, need to be vigilant on the job. Vigilance means watchful, a heightened state of awareness. This state of heightened awareness can be seen in a police officer approaching a car they just stopped in traffic. Vigilance helps them to be prepared for anything that could happen. Vigilance releases adrenaline, which is needed to narrow the officer's focus, just like a lion stalking its prey.

Working in a profession where vigilance is a job requirement can lead to being continually "on guard" even away from work. As this continues, it can become problematic, leading to various physical and mental health issues. To either prevent or address current health problems, as the medical websites say, you will need to work on turning off your emotions.

I want to briefly touch on low-energy negative emotions before moving on. These emotions have a very different effect on our brain, body, and health. These emotions include, but are not limited to, depression, sadness, grief, rejection, discouragement, and disappointment to name a few. Our focus for now will be on the high-energy negative emotions.

# Emotions Have to Be Shut Off

*"I don't want to be at the mercy of my emotions.
I want to use them, to enjoy them, and to dominate them."*
-Oscar Wilde

You have learned that the acute stress response does not shut off automatically like the way fight-or-flight does. Emotions can linger long after what created them is over. Maybe you can think of someone who was still angry about something days after it happened. Maybe it was you.

## What Prolongs Emotional Reactions?

*Type of or Degree of the Emotion.* One reason that emotions stay turned on longer than they need to is based on the initial reaction a person has to what occurred. Emotional energy varies based on the type of emotion you feel.

If we compare two different emotions such as being irritated to feeling angry, which emotion do you think would result in a higher level of negative energy?

Anger will register at a greater level of intensity than irritation, but lower than rage. Irritation, along with annoyance or frustration, is considered to be on the low end of the anger scale. Irate and rage are on the high end. Anger fits within a family of emotions.

Second, the energy of emotion varies by degrees. A question that therapists might ask people is based on the Likert Scale of 1 to 10, what number is your stress right now? This helps to determine the strength of an emotion. The higher the number, the stronger they are feeling the emotion.

The type of emotion you feel and the level of intensity you feel translates into longer periods of time being necessary to calm yourself down to a pre-emotional state. Pre-emotional state means how you felt before you experienced the emotion.

One of the ways you can take control over your emotions is by learning to lower the intensity level of your emotional reaction. Realize that every time you get angry, it should not register at an eight or nine on the anger scale. If you lower the level of your initial emotional reaction from an eight to a six, you will find you shorten the amount of time it takes to recover and calm down.

A person can also change the type of emotion they initially feel. To do this you first need to ask yourself if it is necessary for "you to feel this way." You can become so used to getting angry over everything that you bypass all the lesser emotions such as being irritated, annoyed, or frustrated. These emotions are less intense than anger, easier to control, and therefore quicker to get over. Ask yourself if you really need to be angry every time you react; can you just be annoyed or irritated instead?

The same is true for stress. I know that this is an exaggeration at some level, but we react in a similar way emotionally to a big problem as we do to a little one, to a small irritation as we do to a big one. Not all problems are created equal. Some really are much smaller in size. Quit reacting to situations as if they are the end of the world. It is not, and all crises are not equal! Learning to change the type of emotion you initially feel, combined with lowering the level of intensity of the emotion are great starting steps in learning how to control emotions.

## What Happens During or After Experiencing an Emotion?

You may not realize that how you react to something that is happening to you, or what you do after the incident is over, can keep your emotions turned on longer than they need to be. W. Doyle Gentry in his book Anger Management for Dummies cites a study of eighth-grade students who became angry, what they did afterward, and how it affected the amount of time it took for them to calm down afterward.

It was found that the students who did not engage verbally with the other person at the time of the incident and walked away were able to calm down quicker than those who chose to argue with the other person. (1)

It has long been thought that venting anger could be helpful. It was eventually found that venting emotionally causes a person to stay focused on their emotion longer, not get over it. Engaging in conflict intensifies the emotion you feel during the incident. It increases the length of time the emotion continues afterward. Reacting to the situation hinders your ability to calm down.

Think of a time where you were upset with someone and chose to walk away instead of arguing. Compare that experience to a time when you chose to argue with the other person. Based on your own experience, which one of the ways you responded took you longer to calm down?

This is similar to putting a fire out versus throwing gas on it. Removing yourself from the situation helps put the fire out, while arguing with someone throws gas on it, escalating the emotional fire within you.

A second behavior that keeps the adrenaline flowing and emotion turned on is "telling your story to others" after the situation is over. Once you leave the situation that made you angry, instead of taking the time to calm down, you find someone to tell your story to. Retelling your story causes you to re-experience the emotion and the negative energy that it created.

I am sure you have seen something similar to this with someone you know. When they were retelling a story of something that had just happened to them, you could see and hear the emotions they felt as they told their story. You may have experienced this yourself.

You may have seen this take place at work. Someone has had a negative emotional experience with the boss and then proceeds down the hallway telling others their story. Not only does the negative emotion and energy continue for them, but the negativity they bring with them also begins to spread and infect others. You need to ask yourself if you want to continue retelling the story if it is going to keep you focused on the negative experience and energy that came with it? You may need to learn how to quit listening to others share their negative experiences. It rubs off.

Learning how to step out of the situation that caused the negative emotion is a great way to start controlling your emotions. To get over your emotions quickly means to stop retelling the story that caused them.

## How You Think After the Incident

Some people are able to move on rather quickly after an emotional reaction. Others have difficulty letting it go. Not being able to let things go is usually caused by rumination. Rumination is a term used to describe how a cow chews the cud. They swallow it, spit it back up, and then chew on it some more.

Rumination is when you continue to think about what happened to you in a negative way after the situation is over. When a person is unwilling to let go of what happened to them, they begin to ruminate, continually thinking about it. I would hear this with the adolescents I worked with. "I am not going to let them get away with that," as if some great, world-shaking thing had happened to them. It hadn't.

Instead, they play a conversation in their head over and over about what happened. "Look at how they treated me." "I should have told them off." "I cannot let them get away with that." "What are people going to think about me if I do not do something?" And on and on it goes.

Rumination throws gas on your mental fire as you continue repeating the thoughts. This keeps the memory of the incident alive. You cannot seem to stop the thoughts from coming, which in turn keeps your emotions turned on. Rumination is a big problem with stress.

The funny thing is that when something happens that requires your immediate attention you can temporarily suspend the ruminations. Once you finish the task that called you away, you chose to spit the memory back up like a cow chewing on the cud. You begin to go over it again. Rumination is wasted mental and emotional energy.

To control an emotion, you have to stop the repetitious thoughts and ruminations. If you are thinking about how to solve the problem that caused you to react, great, then figure it out and move on. Do not keep going over the situation in your head and do nothing about it. If you are thinking about how to approach someone to address an issue, then it is a good thing to think it through. But if you are not doing it for these reasons then stop. Stopping your ruminations is a big step forward in controlling your emotions. Stopping your ruminations is a choice you make.

## Another Incident Occurs

When I did the Manage Your Emotions presentation for the juvenile probation officers, I used a Snow Globe to illustrate what happens when adrenaline is released into the bloodstream. I would shake up the Snow Globe and then we would watch the glitter float around.

The glitter represents the release of adrenaline created by an emotional response. The glitter would eventually fall back to the bottom. But before the glitter would completely settle down, I would shake the globe again, representing that another emotional reaction has occurred.

In real life, this happens often. It can start off by leaving the house late for work. Now you are in a hurry, just a little stressed. Traffic is backed up on the expressway due to an accident and there is no way out, a new stressor. You get to work and before you can settle down in your chair, the boss calls you into their office because of a failed deadline. More stress.

With each new stressor, more adrenaline and cortisol are released into the bloodstream. This type of reaction is not limited to stress on top of stress, it can be any combination of negative emotions one after another.

One person I talked with shared how they had received some distressing news about a friend of theirs who was diagnosed with a life-threatening disease. This person felt sadness for their friend as a result. They also felt some anger because life can feel unfair at times. Later that day while driving home and before they could get over their emotional reaction to the bad news, they were involved in an incident with a rude driver. The result of the driving incident caused them to feel a level ten on the anger scale.

They had experienced one emotional incident followed by a second one before having time to process and settle down from the first one. Like the snow globe glitter, the adrenaline from the earlier emotion had not settled to the bottom before it was shaken again. Because they had not completely recovered from the earlier incident, their emotional reaction in the vehicle incident was probably more intense than it would have been under normal circumstances.

A prior negative emotional reaction can cause you to be more emotionally sensitive in future situations. The more negative emotions you experience during the day, the longer adrenaline remains in your bloodstream making it more difficult to calm down. It is important that you deal with each emotion as it comes, and the quicker the better. When your emotions are under control, the better prepared you are to handle the next emotional crisis when it comes.

# The Emotional Barbell

## Brain and Body
## Emotion I----------------v----------------I Behavior
## Hormones > Adrenaline and Cortisol

The emotional barbell helps to visualize how an emotional reaction works. The first part of a barbell is a long round piece of strong metal in the middle. The metal bar represents the interaction between the brain and the release of the hormones adrenaline and cortisol, and the physiological changes that take place.

Weights are attached on each end and are evenly distributed on the barbell. These weights represent emotions on one end and the behavior that comes with emotion on the other. The release of adrenaline creates a feeling of energy in our body we call an emotion on the left side of the barbell. The emotion results in behavior as represented on the right side of the barbell.

## Emotions and Behavior Are Congruent

When a person puts twenty-five pounds on one side of the barbell, they will also need to put twenty-five pounds on the other side of the barbell for it to balance. Without the weight being evenly distributed, the barbell will not be effective for exercising. In an emotional reaction, the weights represent a balance between the emotion on one end and the behavior that follows on the other.

Any emotion felt on one side of the barbell translates into some type of behavior on the opposite end. All emotions result in behavior. Unless you consciously decide to break the emotion-behavior connection to change your behavior, the emotional pattern and behavior that follows will continue as your normal emotional response.

Emotions and the behavior that comes with them are congruent. Congruent is defined as *in agreement with*, or *in harmony*. Congruent means that emotion is in agreement with the behavior that results. When a person feels a certain emotion like anger, the behavior should be what we expect to see when someone is angry. If a person says that they are angry and are smiling and laughing, we're not going to take them seriously. It is not congruent.

The principle of congruency is used to diagnose mental health disorders like depression and anxiety. Mental health disorders come with a checklist of symptoms that are seen in the person's behavior. The behavior has to be *in agreement* with the symptoms that come with the diagnosis. This is true in medicine also. An illness is identified by its symptoms. When a person is diagnosed with a physical illness, or with clinical depression or anxiety, they have to meet the criteria needed for a diagnosis.

There are two forms of depression. One is clinical and the other is situational. Situational depression does not rise to the level needed for a clinical diagnosis. Situational depression still comes with a list of symptoms that can be identified as being congruent with what the person is feeling. Situational depression means there is a current or ongoing event that led to what the person is feeling. Situational depression is a common experience.

The context for the word situational means the problem is temporary and is usually resolved over time. Whether it is clinical or situational depression, the behavior that comes with it will be congruent with how they are feeling.

## Emotions Are Predictable

The behavior that comes with an emotion is predictable. This should not be surprising since we know that emotions and behavior are congruent. Congruent does not mean that everyone who experiences a certain emotion will manifest the same behaviors, in exactly the same way, as another person would. Neither will a person exhibit every behavior that comes with that emotion.

Each emotion comes with a range of behaviors attached to it. Although not everyone will act the same, they will act within an expected range of behaviors that come with that emotion, making emotional behavior predictable.

Most everyone raises their voice when they are angry. But not everyone yells or screams, cusses, calls names, or makes threats. All these behaviors though are within a range of expected behavior when a person is angry. Some people may hit or kick something, punch a hole in a wall, throw or break something, or hit someone. But many people do not do any of these things when they are angry. However, all these behaviors are considered congruent with anger. You understand my point; we know what anger looks like.

Since we know what types of behaviors come with an emotion, we can predict to some degree how a person will act when they feel angry. Knowing each emotion comes with a range of behavior makes behavior predictable in a general way.

Emotions are predictable at an individual level too. Although people engage in some of the same behaviors that others do when they become angry, there will also be differences in how one person behaves versus another, what they will do and will not do. Our emotions come with a set of personalized behavior attached to them.

One of my job responsibilities at juvenile court was to do violence risk assessments on youth who were arrested for some form of violence including threats. Although you can never say with one hundred percent confidence something will or will not happen, you can say with a high level of confidence what you think will happen if you have the right information. The purpose of a violence risk assessment was to determine if a youth was at risk to act violently if they were allowed to return home, to school, or into the community.

In doing a risk assessment, there was specific information I needed to get to determine the adolescent's risk level. After gathering the information I needed, I could make an educated determination of risk. I use this example to emphasize that if the behavior is not predictable at an individual level, then a risk assessment becomes useless. Fortunately, behavior more often than naught can be predicted at a high level.

This principle can be carried over to predicting how a person will behave when they experience certain emotions. The funny thing is that people around you, who know you well, already know how you will behave when you feel a particular emotion. If you were to ask them, they would be able to describe your emotional behavior with a pretty fair degree of accuracy. If you are truthful with yourself, you know how you behave when you experience specific emotions.

To stretch this point a little further, people play out emotions as if they were acting out a movie script. We see people do this all the time in the movies. Good actors are experts at acting out emotions in movies that they are not really feeling. But we believe their emotional performance if they act in a way we expect.

Each one of us is like an actor who knows how to play the part that comes with an emotional reaction. When the time comes to react, we know what to do. Over time our emotions and behavior become automatic like in Fight-or-Flight. We do not have to think about how we will behave when we feel a particular emotion, we simply act out the behavior that comes with that emotion.

Every emotion you have comes with your own personal and predictable behavior. Understanding this makes it easier for you to identify the behavior you need to change. Although emotional behavior is automatic, controlling and changing it will take effort.

# 4

# The Consequences of Not Controlling Your Emotions

*"It's not stress that kills us; it's our reaction to it."*
-Hans Selye

One of the life lessons people have difficulty learning is that choices and behavior lead to consequences. Why do I say that? Because I see adults and juveniles who make the same mistakes over and over again, suffering the same negative consequences of their choices. There is no getting around this life principle that has been expressed in other ways such as you reap what you sow, what goes around comes around, and karma.

Sometimes consequences are immediate, while at other times they are delayed. Some people think they can escape from them, but consequences always catch up to us.

The fact that behavior leads to consequences, good and bad, escapes many of the teenagers I worked with. It is simply not in the way they think. When they decide to do something, they do it and then are surprised when things do not go the way they planned. Some adults think like this too, and their behavior shows it.

Magical thinking is believing that the law of consequences does not apply to you. Teenagers may think about consequences at times, but only for a minute. If they do include consequences in their thinking, they chose to believe they will not get caught and thereby avoid the consequences. Unfortunately, sometimes they do get away with it, which reinforces their negative thinking.

The anger management and corrective thinking classes I conducted for probation youth focused on connecting their choices and behavior to their current consequences. Once a person takes ownership of the choices they make and accept the consequences they are suffering, then the process of change can begin.

Corrective thinking is meant to help people think before they act, think through what they want to do before they do. Most all of us have acted before thinking about the potential consequences of a choice we made. As a result, we made life far more difficult for ourselves than we needed to. It could have been in something as simple as going out with someone you had second thoughts about dating or marrying. Making bad choices where we do not weigh out the consequences should only happen occasionally. If we fail to learn from the consequences we suffer in life, then we are foolish people indeed. Being aware of what could happen can be a great deterrent to making a bad choice.

Being aware of consequences keeps most people from stealing in a store or breaking into a home. How many of you would take a chance to steal from a store if you did not have the money to buy what you wanted? Thinking about what could happen to you is a great deterrent for bad behavior.

Although people are aware that bad choices can end in bad consequences, they may not spend much time, if any, thinking about those consequences before they act. This is also true when it comes to the bad behavior that comes with a person's emotions. Most of you are aware of how your negative emotions can end in bad behavior but is that awareness enough to cause you to stop that behavior before you act on it.

What follows in this chapter is not meant to be a comprehensive look at the potential health consequences that can develop, or that can be exacerbated by negative emotions like stress. It is only meant to serve as a warning of what can develop in the future. I liken this chapter to a yellow flashing light that tells you to be cautious; uncontrolled emotions can lead to a variety of problems that could have been avoided.

## Choices and Behavior Lead to Consequences

Choices lead to behavior. Behavior ends in consequences, period. There is always an end result. Although you do not always think about the potential consequences of your choices and behavior, consequences come anyway. I know firsthand that many teenagers do what they want to do, and if something bad happens, they tell themselves they will deal with it later. Adults too.

There was a commercial on TV years ago that featured a mechanic who said that you could pay him now (for preventative maintenance) or pay him later (for repairs). Higher consequences. Negative emotions and bad behavior have a price tag attached to them.

I remember a client who I believed had an anger problem. Each time he would come into my office he would become angry as different issues were discussed. This continued for several weeks. My client tended to blame either the circumstances in his life or other people, even his family, for his anger.

I decided it was time to do an intervention to specifically talk about his anger. At the next session, when I asked about his anger, he denied he had a problem. I talked with him about how uncontrolled anger can lead to health issues, even precipitate a heart attack. He said that there was nothing to be concerned about and left my office angry again. I received a call from his family about a month later. They said he had experienced a heart attack precipitated by his anger. He quickly became aware that he needed to make some lifestyle changes, especially in learning how to control his anger.

Uncontrolled, high-energy negative emotions, like stress and anger, can precipitate a health crisis.

## Negative Emotions and Physical Health Problems

The dedication in Dr. Mark Hymen's book, Blood Sugar Solutions reads; *"For the first generation of children in history who will live sicker and die younger than their parents. For their sakes and ours may we all work together to take back our health"* (2). In case you missed it, read it again. How you are living today has a payoff tomorrow. Dr. Hyman's quote was used at the start of the Manage Your Emotions presentation for the probation officers.

My purpose was to get their attention at the start of the class on the seriousness of uncontrolled stress. Dr. Hyman's book looks at the reasons we are experiencing a health epidemic related to diabetes, and what you can do to make changes in your life to improve your health.

You will find the usual suspects for many of our health problems, poor nutrition, lack of exercise, and obesity. People can miss how an inability to control stress can lead to health problems. The combination of these different factors has become a flashpoint for a major health crisis in America.

I am not advocating that uncontrolled emotion by itself will be the cause of health concerns like a heart attack. However, what I do know is that many times a lack of emotional control can become the trigger for a health crisis. Negative emotions are closely linked to poor lifestyle choices such as poor eating habits, lack of exercise, smoking, alcohol and drug use, and being overweight.

My purpose in this chapter is to help you develop an awareness of these health concerns. It is not to provide you with a comprehensive look at these health issues.

## Adrenaline's Relation to Health Problems

In 1975, Dr. Herbert Benson of Harvard Medical School wrote *The Relaxation Response*. His book details how some of the health issues of his day were associated with the acute stress response. His book talks about the rise of heart attacks and stroke that was taking place in America and a connection to stress. His book sounded a warning bell of the potential health issues that were developing and coming down the road if changes were not made in our lifestyles.

Stress can lead to health problems by exacerbating health issues you already have. Remember that the fight-or-flight response is meant to turn on and turn off. Failing to turn off the acute stress response, allowing it to stay on for prolonged periods of time was becoming associated with the health issues Dr. Benson was seeing.

People I know in their mid to late forties are in the early stages of high blood pressure. To correct this, they will need to learn how to make better lifestyle choices, including learning how to control their stress and anger. They will need to develop some positive stress coping abilities to help lower their risk for future health issues.

Medication treats the symptoms of high blood pressure, but it cannot help you control your emotions. As people learn to control their emotions and make healthier lifestyle choices like exercise and nutrition, over time they may be able to control their blood pressure without medication.

Adrenaline stimulates the release of glucose, known as blood sugar. Glucose provides the muscles with the energy needed for a fight-or-flight response. When you combine the amount of blood sugar produced by adrenaline, combined with poor eating choices and the use of alcohol, the risk to develop Type 2 diabetes increases over time.

The onset for these various health problems can begin as early as in the late thirties, into the early forties. We are seeing a dramatic increase in the number of people being diagnosed with Type 2 diabetes in America. Even young children are developing Type

2 diabetes due to poor nutrition, poor eating habits, and a lack of exercise, combined with being overweight.

Based on my experience with kids on probation, added to this deadly mix are the emotional problems that these kids were experiencing growing up. In our nation, we see a continuing rise in the breakup of the family unit, child abuse, domestic violence, financial debt, and unstable home life. How could these emotional difficulties not lead to a potential mental health crisis?

Stress can lead to personal dissatisfaction with your life, which can lead to mental health issues like depression and anxiety.

When I used to teach the anger management class, I tried to warn these teenagers of the potential effects of negative emotions over a long period of time. It was really hard for them to picture their lives twenty to thirty years down the road.

One way I tried to make the connection was to ask if they have ever developed a headache after being angry or stressed. I usually got a few kids to respond they had. I asked if they had experienced neck or back pain after being angry. Neck and lower back pain can result from the tightening of the muscles that come with the release of adrenaline. Some said they had.

Some of the teens reported a loss of sleep due to their anger, stress, and anxiety. All these were early warning signs for them how negative emotions can lead to physical health issues. The point is that although they may not experience a heart attack at their age, they are experiencing the physical effects of their negative emotions. Have you ever considered that some of your health concerns might be related to your inability to control your negative emotions?

Stress: Portrait of a Killer makes the case that chronic stress can damage chromosomes and alter brain chemistry. One area of the brain affected by too much adrenaline is the Hippocampus, which contributes to learning and memory.

Many people have experienced the cause-and-effect relationship of stress on short-term memory. It happens when a person is in a very stressful situation that continues for a period of time. They may find that they are forgetting things, or misplacing items they cannot find later. After the stress passes, so does this period of forgetfulness. Even in this simple example, you can see that stress can have a short-term effect on your memory.

Chronic stress can age you. We have seen this happen by watching the President of the United States' hair turn gray over the four to eight years he is in office. The father of stress research Hans Selye said, "Every stress leaves an indelible scar, and the organism pays for its survival after a stressful situation by becoming a little older." Mr. Selye died in 1982, years before all the medical research could confirm what he believed.

## What About Cortisol?

The second hormone in fight-or-flight, cortisol, can also be damaging to your health. Cortisol suppresses the immune system, which increases the risk for health problems due to turned-on emotions. If your immune system is not operating at peak performance, then you become more vulnerable to developing health issues in the future like Type 2 diabetes, or hyper/hypo thyroidism. Too much cortisol over time can impair the body's ability to fight off an illness or slow down the healing process. When our physiology is hijacked by these two hormones for prolonged periods of time, you can see how the potential for health problems can develop. There are other types of consequences to your brain by the overload of cortisol.

A quick way to illustrate the effects of stress and cortisol is to look at a time when you were under a great deal of stress. For a college student it could be finals week, for you it could be a work project or personal crisis. Once the student's tests are done, the work project completed, and the crisis is over, you get sick. It is a common occurrence. The high level of stress you felt while going through the situation lowered your immune system making you more vulnerable to catching a cold. If increased cortisol levels can make it difficult to fight off something as simple as a cold, think of the effect this can have when battling a major heath concern.

There is more that could be said about the health problems associated with elevated levels of adrenaline and cortisol, but the object here is to show you that you are at risk when you do not control your emotions and your stress response. If you are interested in learning more about health issues and stress, go to your local library and check out the vast resources that are available to you.

## Negative Emotions and Relationship Problems

As a marriage and family therapist, I believe in the helpfulness of counseling. At the same time, I believe that it only works when people are truly motivated to change.

Families go to counseling for a multitude of reasons. But by the time they arrive at the counselor's office, a lot of negative emotions have come and gone, and some of them may have manifested in bad behavior.

Disagreements can be settled, and problems solved, but not when emotions are out of control. Negative emotions break down communication and the ability to solve problems. The inability to communicate effectively damages the relationship and makes it harder to repair it. Emotions and the behaviors that accompany them can cause hurt feelings and deep wounds. Stress and anger can escalate into domestic violence or child abuse.

Prior to these types of things happening, the original problem was probably solvable, and solutions could have been negotiated. When the emotional intensity is high, or violence has occurred, problems become more difficult to resolve, because the relationship has become more strained.

Emotions need to be kept in check if both parties want to talk things out and find solutions for their problems. Sometimes it only takes one person who is willing to change by putting their emotions in check and their pride behind them to restore a relationship.

I do not want to minimize the seriousness of relationship issues. Marriage problems can be complicated, and professional help may be needed. In relationships, we need to get our eyes off the other person, look at ourselves, and see what needs to change in us. There are always improvements we can make in our lives apart from the other person.

Take the responsibility to make yourself happy and your relationship better. Do not wait on the other person to change. You may still need to go to marriage counseling, but then again, if you take control of your life, emotions, and behavior, maybe not! Sometimes when one person changes, it sparks a desire in the other person to change.

Relationship problems cannot be addressed when you are emotionally charged up. If you want your marriage or your relationship with your kids to improve, get your emotions under control and out of the way. Learn how to communicate emotion-free. It will take practice, but it will improve your relationship with others.

One parent I worked with could not understand the importance of emotion-free communication. This parent spoke in a loud voice, which was clearly an indicator of how she communicated at home. This parent tended to talk a lot, interrupt, and not listen to their child when they had something to say. This was a common problem for many parents I counseled.

When I spoke to her about opening up the lines of communication, she made it clear that this is how she communicates and that she was not going to change. Her style was negative, focused on her needs, and filled with emotion. She could not see how her communication style was shutting her child down from wanting to communicate with her.

Negative emotions shut down communication. As the adolescent left my office, they whispered to me, "I can't wait until I am 18 and can get out of my home." Have you ever felt a similar way with someone who communicated with a lot of negative emotion and did not listen to what you had to say? Although this parent felt they were winning the communication battle, she was on the verge of losing the relationship battle.

The point here is how negative emotions can damage a relationship. Take a few minutes before continuing to read and take an inventory of your relationships. Have your negative emotions gotten in the way of your feelings of closeness or your ability to communicate with others, or alienated you from others? If so, I hope you will take the time to reach out and mend the bridge now.

## Negative Emotions Are Personally Destructive

What is the personal cost to you when you lose control of your emotions? Maybe it is the loss of intimacy with a spouse, a divorce, the growing distance between you and your children, loss of a job or friends, substance abuse problems, or an arrest because you lost control when you got angry.

People tend to believe that emotions result from something outside of themselves. When the problem goes away, they will be fine. They think the other person caused me to react this way. This is what the man believed that I was counseling with who had a heart attack.

If you do not like the negative energy you feel, you are the only one who has the power to shut it off. Not liking the way an emotion feels should be a flashing warning signal that says it is time to make a change.

Although we have been talking about high-energy negative emotions caused by adrenaline, low-energy negative emotions such as depression, disappointment, and discouragement can be just as deadly and destructive to your health as the high-energy emotions, but in a different way. We will talk about this later.

# A Biblical Perspective on Emotions

*"He who has knowledge spares his words, and a
man of understanding is of a calm spirit."*
(Proverbs 17:27)

Blaise Pascal, a French mathematician and philosopher said, *"There is a God-shaped vacuum in the heart of every man;"* this quote usually stops here, but the rest of the quote goes on to say, *"which cannot be filled by any created thing, but only by God, the Creator, made known through Jesus."* When you take this point of view, the spiritual dimension becomes very clear and relevant to man's needs. God is man's creator. Man separated from God is incomplete. It is only a belief in God that can explain man's existence, *how he got here,* and significance, *why he is here.*

A spiritual perspective brings meaning and purpose to man's life by pointing beyond his limited existence on earth. Eternity enhances man's significance beyond this lifetime. But the spiritual dimension also brings with it requirements of how you are to handle your emotions, think, behave, and treat other people.

## A Spiritual Point of View

The apostle Paul writes, "Now may the God of peace Himself sanctify you completely; and may your whole spirit, soul, and body be preserved blameless at the coming of our Lord Jesus Christ." (I Thessalonians 5:23). Paul identifies man as being comprised of spirit, soul, and body.

Paul's writings in other New Testament books refer to the body as a house, tent, and temple. A house, tent, and temple are outward forms of buildings. Although the exterior of a building may have aesthetic value, the importance of the building is related to the activity that takes place inside. A home or tent is where people live together, while a temple is a place where people worship together. Tents were common in Biblical times. In Paul's reference, we can see our body as the house for the spirit and soul, as well as the Holy Spirit.

The soul is made up of intellect, emotions, and will. These work together to make up the qualities of who we are, what we refer to as the personality. Our personality is seen in how we talk, act, think, and feel. These qualities, in addition to how we look, make us unique. Our personality with all of its qualities is referred to as the soul. At death, our personality ceases to be in this present world, waiting to be restored in the resurrection at the end of this age.

The third aspect of man's makeup is the spirit. Man's spirit is the gift of life given to him by God. At death man's spirit departs from the body. To understand what Paul is referring to when he uses the term spirit, we must go back to the beginning, the book of Genesis.

## Creation: Where Life Begins

"And the Lord God formed man of the dust of the ground and breathed into his nostrils the breath of life; and man became a living being." (Genesis 2:7.) As a Christian, I believe that the Genesis account offers the only reasonable explanation for the existence of man. It identifies how man arrived on this planet and his purpose for him being here.

No other theory of creation can explain why man exists. They can tell you what they think.

The Bible elevates man's significance by stating we were created in God's image. God's blueprint for creating man is, "So God created man in His own image; in the image of God He created him; male and female He created them." (Genesis 1:27.)

Man's beginnings start with God forming man from the dust of the ground. God begins with dust, shapes a body and bends over this lifeless form, and breathes into it the breath of life. The OT Hebrew word that is used here is ruach. Ruach can be translated as *spirit, wind,* or *breath*.

The New Testament uses the Greek word pneuma for the spirit. Pneuma is translated as *spirit, wind, or breath* just as ruach is in the OT. The use of a capitol R for Ruach, or a capitol P with Pneuma, distinguishes God's Spirit, and the Holy Spirit, from man's spirit. The spirit of man resulted from the breath of God entering into a body that had been fashioned by God. Adam becomes a living being, with a personality.

## The First Mention of Emotions

Most people have heard of Adam and Eve, religious or not. In Genesis God gave a command to man, "but of the tree of the knowledge of good and evil you shall not eat, for in the day you eat of it you shall surely die." (Genesis 2:17.) Apart from this one command, Adam and Eve were pretty much free to do anything they wanted.

Adam and Eve are tempted by the serpent to eat the fruit of the tree Adam was told not to do. Prior to eating the fruit of the tree, Adam and Eve "… were both naked, the man and his wife, and were not ashamed." (Genesis 2:25.) Their relationship as seen through their eyes was pure; naked and unashamed.

It appears in the Genesis account that God would meet at various times with Adam and Eve in the Garden of Eden. One day, something happens that changes everything. Summarizing the story, they eat the fruit, their eyes are opened, they realize they are naked, make clothes from fig leaves, and then try to hide from God's presence when they hear Him walking in the garden.

As God walks through the garden, He calls out to Adam. Adam "… said, "I heard your voice in the garden, and I was afraid because I was naked, and I hid myself." (Genesis 3:10.)

*Fear,* I was afraid. As a result of eating the fruit, they experienced fear for the first time. A fearfulness of God that was not there before they ate the fruit. This fear causes a change in Adam and Eve's behavior toward Him. Prior to this, Adam would have come out to greet God and spend time with Him in the garden. But now Adam hides from Him. Disobedience to God's command not to eat the fruit changes Adam and Eve's behavior.

A second emotion that Adam and Eve's experience is *shame.* Adam and Eve were previously naked and unashamed, but now they cover their bodies with fig leaves because of shame. Shame is an emotion that is expressed as a conscious negative feeling related to having an awareness of doing something wrong. Adam and Eve now feel a need to cover themselves. Man's innocence was lost that day in the garden.

Shame changes how they relate to God. The fig leaves, in addition to covering their shame from each other, also is an attempt to cover their shame from God.

*Fear* is seen in Adam's response to God when he is required to give an account for eating the fruit. Adam is not unlike a child who is caught with his hand in the cookie jar knowing he did something that he was not supposed to do. Adam being afraid blames Eve, and Eve blames the snake. Both Adam and Eve avoid taking the responsibility for their disobedience. Taking responsibility is the only way that a person can make corrections in their life when they have made bad choices. But Adam and Eve avoid taking the responsibility for their behavior.

The Garden of Eden story provides the first look at negative emotions and the bad behavior that comes with those emotions. It reveals that there are consequences that come with bad choices and bad behavior. The Bible provides a historical perspective of the first time when negative emotions became a part of man's history and makeup.

God did not create us for negative emotions. They are clearly a part of man's fallen nature.

## Further Results from the Garden

There is one other thing we need to recognize from the Garden of Eden story before we move on. When God created the earth and all that was in it, He repeatedly said through each step of creation that it was good. But after the creation of man, the final piece of creation, "Then God saw everything He had made, and indeed it was very good..." (Genesis 1:31.)

Man was the crowning glory of creation in a world where all things were perfect and worked together in harmony. It is not until Adam and Eve eat the fruit of the tree that things change, and the harmony of creation is broken. And this not good.

The Garden of Eden incident is referred to as the Fall of Man. Man's fall in the garden becomes the starting point of man's sinful nature. Prior to this, Adam and Eve had been created perfectly. Sin enters creation because of man's disobedience. It is important to note that the manifestation of negative emotions takes place after man's disobedience. These negative emotions were not there prior to this, nor do I believe they were meant to be a part of the original creation.

## The First Mention of Anger

"But God did not respect Cain and his offering. And Cain was very angry, and his countenance fell. So the Lord said to Cain, why are you angry? And why has your countenance fallen?" (Genesis 4:5-6.) The reference to Cain's countenance falling refers to Cain's demeanor, which I believe describes Cain as being either *disappointed, discouraged,* or *depressed.*

The background to this story is that people in the Old Testament, prior to the Law Moses was given in the book of Exodus, people were expected to present offerings to God as a part of their relationship with Him. Although it is not specifically stated in the text, the offering was to be an animal sacrifice. I will not elaborate on this because our focus is on the emotions of the story.

Cain and Able are brothers who bring their offerings to God on a certain day as an act of worship. Abel brings the appropriate sacrifice, a meat offering as required. Cain brings a food offering, a harvest taken from his garden, which is not the appropriate offering to bring. At this point, Cain is not in agreement with God's requirement for the sacrifice.

God responds to Cain, "If you do well, will you not be accepted? And if you do not do well, sin lies at the door. And its desire is for you, but you should rule over it." (Genesis 4:7.) God was trying to tell Cain it was not too late to go and do the right thing. Cain still has time to make the right sacrifice. We do not know whether Cain does this or not since it is not reported as a part of the story. But as you continue reading you get the sense he does not.

The story moves forward in time to when Cain and Abel are walking together in a field. "… Cain rose up against Abel his brother and killed him." (Genesis 4:8.) Although no emotions are specifically mentioned by name in this verse, I want to state that what I believe we see at work in the killing of Abel are *anger,* as mentioned in verse 6, and *jealousy.* I believe that Cain was jealous and angry at his brother because God accepted Abel's offering, but not his. He could also have been angry with God because God did not accept what he felt was a good sacrifice.

Anger and jealousy have gone hand in hand throughout history. These two emotions have been responsible for much of the domestic violence and spousal murder we see in the United States today. Jealousy is a deadly emotion, and when coupled with anger is lethal. Cain chooses to kill his brother. Anger can quickly escalate to violence if it is not held in check.

This is the second example in the Bible of negative emotions and the harmful consequences that result from them. The negative emotions that are identified in these two stories are fear, anger, shame, and jealousy, which all appear after Adam and Eve's disobedience.

There was recently a story in the news of one retired pastor shooting and killing another retired pastor after an argument. The argument was over something that was minor in contrast to the price that was paid, the loss of a man's life. As pastors and brothers in Christ, they should have known how to work out their disagreement, but their emotions took over just as Cain's did with Abel. We need to realize that we can do stupid, even harmful things when we do not control our emotions.

## Spiritual Life and Death

I use the story of Adam and Eve to illustrate the way things were before and after the fall. What happens after Adam and Eve's fall are in direct opposition to what God intended for him. The connection between negative emotions, bad behavior, and the consequences that come with them stand out in these two stories.

The Bible, Old and New Testament, has a lot to say about emotions. It is filled with stories of men and women who had trouble controlling their emotions, the bad behavior that came with them, and the consequences that followed.

An important thing to understand about the fall of man goes back to God creating man in His image. God's image is made up of the attributes and characteristics that are central to who God is. God's image is not represented by an outward form, but by His internal characteristics as represented in His eternal being.

When God created Adam, he was created with the same attributes and characteristics that are central to God's nature. Disobedience led to man losing this image. The fall of man led to three results. The first is God's nature in man was lost. The second is spiritual death, man's relationship with God is cut off. The third is physical death, which follows later.

- **Spiritual Death**. Spiritual death is a loss of a relationship with God. Man has lost his access to God. "And you He made alive who *were* dead in trespasses and sin, in which you once walked." (Ephesians 2:1.) Adam died spiritually at the moment he sinned and felt the consequences immediately. Adam took on a new nature that was at its core sinful. The sinful nature is passed on to Adam's children, "for all have sinned and fall short of the glory of God." (Romans 3:23.) Therefore, we are all spiritually dead until our relationship with God is restored, what is called born again. Although Adam lived for a long period of time after the garden incident, spiritual death was immediate.

- **Spiritual Life Is Only Restored Thru Faith in Jesus**. Man's failure opened the door to God's plan for restoration. Since God is the only one who knows what His original plan for man looked like He is the only one that can restore it. The process of redemption and restoration begins when you believe that Jesus died on the cross for your sins, and in His resurrection on the third day. These beliefs must be followed by a confession that Jesus Christ is the Son of God and by personally accepting Jesus as your savior. In

Christian terminology, you invite Jesus into your heart. Paul says that this results in, "even when we were dead in trespasses, made us alive together with Christ, (by grace you have been saved.)" (Ephesians 2:5.) The confession of Jesus Christ as your savior results in becoming a child of God. "But as many as received him, to them He gave them the right to become the children of God, to those who believe on his name." (John 1:12.)

What man lost in the fall, in addition to his intimacy with God, was the *image of God* in him. Man's original nature was replaced by a sinful nature, which brings self-centeredness, bad behavior, negative emotions, and broken relationships. God's work of restoring man to His original purpose begins with a profession of faith in Jesus Christ.

- **Physical Death Follows Spiritual Death.** "As it is appointed for men to die once, but after this the judgment." (Hebrews 9:27.) This leaves man in a future predicament, judgment. The Bible reveals God's plan for man's salvation, and how man can avoid future judgment. "For God so loved the world that He gave His only begotten son, that whosoever believes in Him will not perish but have everlasting life." (John 3:16.)

In the Genesis account, we see is that emotions, thinking, and bad behavior came with man's fall. As a believer, you need to be aware of how each of these areas affects your relationship with the Father and with man. Fortunately for us, God wants to help us make changes in our life. His desire is to restore His image in you if will believe in His Son Jesus Christ, which includes restoring your relationship with Him and teaching you how to control your emotions and behavior.

# Controlling the Acute Stress Response

## The Acute Stress Response

Immediate Emotional Response > Body's Response > Immediate Behavioral Response

The diagram above represents how the acute stress response works in an emotional reaction. The emotional reaction can be broken into three separate responses: immediate emotional response, physiological response, and immediate behavioral response. The immediate emotional response means the emotions you feel at the present moment. Each response can be examined independently, but it takes all three of these responses working together to create an emotional reaction.

Think for a moment of the many different emotions you experienced this past week. Were there any times you failed to control your emotional reactions the way you needed to? The first step of change begins with controlling the physiological response that was created when the amygdala reacted to the external stimulus.

## Controlling My Body's Response

The physiological response results from the release of adrenaline and cortisol into your bloodstream. The physiological response increases your heart rate, which speeds up the circulation of adrenaline throughout your body. As long as the physiological response is turned on, you will continue to experience the emotion and the negative energy that comes with it. The first step in learning how to control an emotional reaction begins with reversing the physiological response, shutting it down.

We touched on the relaxation response in chapter five when we looked at the health problems connected to stress. The relaxation response covers a group of activities that are used to reverse fight-or-flight. This response can be practiced on an ongoing basis to give you a greater sense of peace in your life. These activities include finding a quiet place, progressive muscle relaxation, visualization, and controlled breathing. Practicing the relaxation response will help to counteract the physiological changes created by high-energy negative emotions like stress. The relaxation response can also lead to positive health benefits and a more tranquil life.

A couple of years after reading Dr. Benson's book, a friend of mine encouraged me to try yoga as a part of my regular workout routine. After a period of resistance, I gave in and gave it a shot. Following the first yoga session, I felt relaxed and de-stressed. The yoga workout was much harder than I had imagined, but the benefits I felt were immediate. Susi, our yoga instructor, would begin each class with breathing exercises to teach us how to breathe properly during the workout.

Having read The Relaxation Response, I knew that breathing helped to lower blood pressure and control stress. I began to practice the yoga breathing technique I had learned as I went through my day at work. Over time, I found my blood pressure was lowering, I was less emotionally reactive, and felt more relaxed at the end of the day. Finding times during the day where you can quiet yourself and practice breathing for a few minutes can go a long way in helping to control your emotions.

## Yoga Breathing = Controlled Breathing

Yoga breathing gives you the ability to control your breathing, thereby lowering your heart rate. This shuts off the flow of adrenaline into your body. Controlling your breathing is necessary for controlling a negative emotional reaction.

## Yoga Breathing Technique

- Breathing is done through the nose. This gives you greater control over the amount of air you breathe in and out.
- Breathing is slow and steady.
- Breathing is a slow four-count followed by a one-count pause. The count should go like this, one, and a two, and a three, and a four, pause.
- Continue to breathe in for all four counts. Do not stop breathing in until you hit pause. Then stop and hold your breath. Now repeat this as you breathe out.
- Breathe from your core. Your belly should rise with each breath and then deflate as you breathe out. As your belly fills with air, your chest will begin to rise. As you breathe out your belly and chest will deflate.
- Breathing continues for two to three minutes. Longer if needed. As you practice yoga breathing, you will find it takes less time for you to calm down.
- Close your eyes if you are at a place where you can do this. This will help you focus on breathing.
- As you breathe, become aware that the emotional energy is dissipating.

- Continue to breathe until you return to a pre-fight-or-flight state of calm.

Yoga breathing is the first, and the most important step in learning how to control your emotional responses. To control the physiological response, you must shut off the adrenaline, which yoga breathing does. It is also the simplest step to take because everyone can learn how to yoga breathe. The only thing you have to do is make a choice to breathe.

## Breathing Helps You Refocus

The benefit of breathing is generally focused on slowing the heart rate to help a person calm down. There is a second benefit that is just as important in learning to control your emotions.

Going back to the physiological changes that take place during fight-or-flight is that focus narrows. The animal is focused on one thing only, survival. When focus narrows to this extent the animal develops tunnel vision. The animal is not aware of anything else except its survival.

An emotional reaction produces a narrowed focus. In an emotional reaction, your focus is on who or what caused the reaction and what you are going to do about it. It is like hitting your thumb with a hammer. The only thing you are thinking about at that moment is the pain you feel. The behavior that follows is instantaneous. That is how emotions work.

Hitting your thumb can result in jumping up and down, combined with a little cussing. The behavioral response that takes place when you hit your thumb is similar to what happens when you feel an emotion. The behavioral response happens quickly, especially when you get angry and your focus narrows.

When your focus narrows and your thoughts race, you are *no longer thinking in a normal or rational way*, similar to the people on

Maple Street. For lack of a better word, you are in *emotional think*. Emotional thinking is programmed thinking that leads to people doing and saying stupid things. In an emotional reaction, you can lose the ability to think rationally.

To regain control of an emotional reaction you must be able to stop the racing thoughts, expand your ability to see the big picture, and bring your thinking back to a calm state. Controlled breathing gives you the power to slow down the racing thoughts, expand your focus, and increase your ability to think.

## Breathing and Muscle Tension

Another physiological change that takes place in fight-or-flight is that muscles tense up. Muscle tension is important to the zebra because it needs to be prepared to outrun the lion. Adrenaline prepares the zebra's muscles to run. The kids in my anger management classes were familiar with the muscle tension they feel when they get angry or even stressed out. This muscle tension is expressed in their body as they begin to make a fist or clench their teeth before they lash out.

As a person calms down there is a release in muscle tension. To see how breathing can relieve muscle tension try this out. Stand up, bend over from your hips, and reach for your toes. Keep your legs and back straight as you can as you bend over. Do not hunch your back. When you come to a point where you are no longer able to bend further, stop. You should be able to feel some tension in your lower back and down your legs. Become aware of the tension and tightness you feel.

As you hang there, slowly do three to four rounds of yoga breathing. As you breathe notice that your muscles start to relax, and the tension lessens. After you stop breathing, see if you can bend over a little further. You should be able to do so.

How did this happen? Breathing allowed a lessening of the tension you felt in your legs and back that was created by stretching.

Once the tension lessened, you were able to bend over a little further. Breathing can help you relieve the tension in your muscles created by stress. Breathing is a key to reversing the physiological changes that come with the acute stress response.

## Controlling the Immediate Emotional Response

Controlling the body's physiological response is the first step in learning to control the immediate emotion you feel. The diagram above indicates that the physiological response occurs almost simultaneously with the emotional response. Cutting off the adrenaline will take the energy out of any high-energy negative emotional reaction. It is similar to letting the air out of a balloon.

As the negative energy and emotional tension lessen, you will find that you are back in control before you felt the emotion minutes ago. When the emotional energy dissipates you can make a much wiser choice of how you want to behave.

Many anger management programs teach people that the first thing they need to do is to remove themselves from the situation that caused them to become angry. They are encouraged to go for a walk, or to a place where they can calm down and clear their thoughts. This is good advice. Leaving a situation is always a smart choice and lessens the chance a person will behave inappropriately. If you need to get out of an emotional situation, then get out. Once you do though, find a place to breathe and calm down.

Learning to control the physiological response of emotion becomes the perfect time to put your focus on the negative energy you feel. When you feel this energy tell yourself you do not want to feel this way, and then breathe.

Even when the emotional energy is gone, you may still have thoughts about the situation that caused you to react. This is normal. The emotional intensity you first felt may have been a nine or ten, but by breathing it has lowered to a two or three. When the emotional intensity has died down, you are in a better position to make better choices about what you are going to do.

The difficulty some people have is deciding whether they want to let the emotion go and move on, or to hold on to the emotion for whatever reason. Remember how long it took those eighth-grade kids to calm down because they continued arguing with others. I found that when probation kids were willing to walk away from the situation or a person that led to their reaction, they could calm down, and almost all of them would let the situation go.

They were able to realize some things are not that big of a deal or worth holding on to. This clearly reveals that there are two possible ways of thinking at work in emotional reactions. One way of thinking takes place while we are emotionally reacting. The other takes place once we are able to calm down and think.

Once you control the physiological response caused by the emotion, it is less likely there will be a behavioral response. A behavioral response always follows on the heels of the emotion you feel. It is the last link in the emotional reaction chain. When you are in control of the emotion, you will be in control of how you behave.

The emotional, physiological, and immediate behavioral responses are linked together like a chain-link fence in an emotional reaction. Changing one response will have a positive effect on changing the other two responses. We will look at controlling the immediate behavioral response in more detail in the next chapter.

## A Story about the Power of Breathing

I received a call in my office from the secretary that one of the adolescents who had arrived for their weekly visit was having a problem in the waiting room and needed help. As I approached the young man it was clear he was beginning to have a panic attack.

I asked him to walk with me to the restroom so he could put some cold water on his face and calm down. As he stood at the sink his legs began to buckle. I quickly sat him down on the floor and then joined him.

As we sat there, I asked him to look at me and breathe at the same pace I was breathing. When his head would drop down, I would gently lift his chin to make eye contact again. I continued to say to him, "Breathe with me." My breathing was slow and steady. I wanted him to synch his breathing with mine. This was meant to help him slow down his rapid breathing so he could slow down his heart rate.

Within a couple of minutes, he had calmed down as his breathing returned to normal. Within just a few short minutes he was able to regain his composure and enter my office for a session. The key to controlling his panic attack was to slow down his heart rate by breathing.

It is also important to note that in a panic attack the person's thoughts are racing and they are narrowly focused on what they are experiencing. It is hard for them to think about anything else. As his breathing slowed, his thoughts stopped racing and he was able to refocus.

We did a few counseling sessions that included teaching him how to yoga breathe in case he experienced another panic attack in the future. I wanted him to understand that by controlling his breathing he had the power to control his heart rate and stop the panic attack, refocus, and regain control.

Panic attacks can be caused when a person is in stress overload and feels overwhelmed. This young man felt he needed to help provide for his family who was having financial difficulties at the time. His father and mother had been out of work for a period of time and there were younger siblings at home. In addition, he had school and job responsibilities at just eighteen years of age. He wanted to help his family by contributing financially.

This was a common situation in the homes of many of the kids I worked with. Although their intentions were admirable, they were not mentally or emotionally ready to take on responsibilities such as these. Carrying the responsibilities for taking care of a family is difficult for adults at times; how much for more an eighteen-year-old teenager.

When he felt overwhelmed the panic attack would manifest. As a way to cope with his stress, he would use marijuana, but the marijuana created an additional stressor for him because it conflicted with his probation responsibilities of not using drugs. Drug use increased his risk of being arrested, which increased the level of stress he was already feeling.

Teaching him yoga breathing would help him control the panic attacks in the future. What will need to happen is for him to learn ways to control the stress in his life before it gets to where he feels overwhelmed. He will need to make certain lifestyle changes, learn some problem-solving skills, and balance what he can and cannot do for his family. This young man is no different from many people I know who struggle with anxiety and stress due to trying to juggle the responsibilities of life and family. Breathing is a powerful weapon in learning how to control your emotional reactions and keep them in check.

# Controlling the Immediate Behavioral Response

"I think I can, I think I can, I think I can"
-The Little Train that Could

In the first step of change, we saw how the three responses are interwoven—emotions affect behavior, thinking affects emotions and behavior, and emotions can have an impact on our thinking. In the second step of change, we will separate the immediate behavioral response from the emotion you felt.

You have learned that emotional behavior is congruent, predictable, and comes with a set of personalized behaviors attached to it. Because this is true, you should already be aware of any negative behavior that you need to stop and change that comes with the emotion you have decided to work on.

Quick example: what is your behavior when getting angry? Do you cuss at others when you get angry? Anger can let the monster out. So even when you feel angry and want to cuss, you can stop the behavior while still feeling angry. This is what it means to separate one response from the other two.

Emotional-behavioral responses are programmed responses. These responses work at a non-conscious level meaning they are not consciously thought through before acting on them. The behavioral response takes over as the emotional response continues. Changing emotional behavior requires you to focus on the behavior while ignoring how you feel at the moment.

## Changing Reinforced Behavior

Behavior created by an emotion tends to be repetitious. This is true for fight-or-flight behavior, run or fight. With emotions, just like in fight-or-flight, most people do not stop and think about what they are going to do. The zebra will always run away from the lion, unless something drastic changes, like a need to protect its young. Although the zebra will lose every time it has to face a lion, the zebra's behavior only changes if something greater happens that causes it to override the animal's need to survive.

Think for a moment about the zebra's change of behavior. What can this teach you about changing your behavior? If a zebra has the ability to override its natural instinct to run, what does that say about your ability to override your emotions and control your behavior? If an animal can do this, surely you have the ability to control and change your behavior.

Ivan Pavlov, a Russian physiologist, conducted a famous experiment that showed how animal—which also translates to human—behavior can be conditioned by an external stimulus. In Pavlov's experiment, a dog's feeding time was combined with the ringing of a bell. Under normal circumstances, a dog naturally salivates when food is given to it. Now, a bell will ring each time food is given to the dog. Over time, the dog is conditioned to salivate when the bell rings, believing food is coming even when no food is present.

A quick example of this can be seen in how a person responds when they find a letter in their mailbox from the IRS. What emotion would you feel? This is no different than the dog responding to the bell.

Pavlov then reversed the experiment. This time the bell would ring each day without bringing food to the dog. Over time, the dog quit salivating to the sound of the bell. The dog's conditioned behavior, salivating to the sound of the bell, was extinguished when no food was brought to it.

What this experiment teaches us at a practical level is that behavior, whether good or bad, can be conditioned to respond in a repetitive pattern by an outside stimulus. The repetitive pattern of how you respond will continue until you choose to change it.

This principle also applies to the conditioned responses of your emotional reactions. Conditioned means *reinforced* or *programmed* into your behavior and emotions. The good news is that behavior that has been programmed can be extinguished or deprogrammed.

Fight-or-flight, run or fight, is exactly how programmed emotional behavior works. Pick any emotion you struggle with and then look at how quickly you behave. Your emotional behavior is no different from Pavlov's dog salivating to the bell.

## Conditioned, Reinforced, and Programmed Behavior

Repetitious behavior forms a neural pathway in the brain, leading to a conditioned response. This is also true for repetitive emotions. This pathway allows a person to respond quicker, just like an animal in fight or flight. The neural pathway helps your brain to be efficient.

Efficiency means that when you are in a situation where you need to respond quickly, you will not have to take the time to think through what you are going to do. Brain efficiency helps you determine what you need to do quickly.

Programmed emotional responses can create problems for us since the brain does not differentiate between what is a good or bad emotional reaction regarding behavior at the time. Punching a person in the face or walking away from an argument when you are angry, are responses created by how the brain has been programmed to respond. The brain response follows a pathway that you created based on how you have responded in the past. The brain does not evaluate your emotional-behavioral response as to whether it is good or bad, appropriate or inappropriate at the moment. Although your brain does not do this during a typical emotional reaction, you may feel differently after the situation when you have had time to think.

The reason people behave stupidly when they are angry, like saying something they cannot take back, or hurting someone physically is because their behavior has been programmed over time. A problem can arise when the behavior starts escalating.

Once the behavior is programmed to respond in certain ways, how do we change this?

This leads us back to Pavlov's experiment. The great news for you and me is all responses, behavioral and emotional, can be deprogrammed and thus changed. Any behavioral response, no matter how engrained it has become, can be changed, even extinguished. This is true for your emotional responses too.

I would like to use a simple yet familiar example to illustrate programmed behavior. The person standing in line next to you sneezes. What do you do?

I am willing to bet you thought the words, "bless you" or "God bless you." It's instantaneous and automatic. At some point in time, you were taught that this was the right way to respond to this situation. You were not expecting someone to sneeze, but once it happens, you know what to do.

Maybe you did not say it because you thought someone else would do it. Maybe you have said bless you in the past, but you have decided to stop saying it. To be able to overcome the programmed response, the urge to say bless you, a choice has to be made not to say it. If you stop doing it enough times you can break the connection between a sneeze and your response.

This is true for all behavior. Deprogramming behavior begins with the awareness to catch the behavior before you act, and work on stopping it every time. As you continue to stop the behavior before you act, like Pavlov's dog, the behavior will be extinguished.

Deprogramming behavior begins with an awareness of the behavior you want to change. If you want to stop yelling, screaming, cussing, making threats, hitting, or throwing things when you become angry, you will need to be aware you behave like this before you can change it.

I have worked with people who learned how to stop their bad behavior in the middle of heated conflict. I have seen this demonstrated with adults and adolescents alike who have a history of violence. Although they may still have a serious problem controlling their anger at times, they have learned how to stop the violence that has led to them being arrested in the past.

The ability to control their behavior came as a result of learning to think differently about their behavior. They need to think about the consequences before they act. The best way to do this was to help them visualize being arrested again and going back to jail if they acted out. With this visual image planted in their subconscious, it was easier to change their thinking about using violence in the future. When understanding the consequences of future behavior sank in, it helped change their thinking going forward.

I have seen a similar thing happen at work. A person who feels angry toward their boss understands the need to control the urge to yell at them. But if they get upset with a coworker, they might yell at them not fearing the consequences.

These two different work situations demonstrate that a person has the ability to pick and choose if their emotional behavior will be let loose or restrained. This is similar to the zebra changing its behavior to protect her young from the lion. Just because you feel a certain way, does not mean you have to act a certain way. You have the ability to control and change any emotional behavior.

The thoughts the men had when they became angry that led to them being arrested had been replaced by new thoughts; "I do not want to go to jail," or "I do not want to lose my job." These new thoughts were able to replace deeply engrained emotional behavior. Their new way of thinking helped them to override the urge to act out even while they were angry.

## After-During-Before

Changing emotional behavior begins by interrupting the behavior in your thinking before you act out. This is similar to a boxing match when the referee steps in between two fighters who are holding on to each other. His purpose for doing this is to free them up so they can start boxing again.

Interrupting your behavior means you are breaking it away from the emotion it is attached to. This allows you to make a better choice of how you want to behave. Since emotional behavior is automatic for the most part, you have to interrupt the thought process to change the behavior.

I remember taking a speech class in college in which one of my speeches was videotaped. As I watched the video, I became embarrassed at how many times I said, "you know." The longer the speech went on the more times I said, "you know." It became painful to hear those two words.

I worked hard to make sure those two words would not come out of my mouth during my next speech. When the opportunity came, I felt prepared to control those two words. Each time I began to say, "you know," I was quickly reminded not to say those words. Because of this, I was able to catch myself before the words came out of my mouth. The speech went much better and was less distracting for those listening. Putting the thought to stop saying those two words into my conscious stream of thought helped me to eliminate the behavior.

When you give your brain a message (we will talk more on this later) to remind you about something you want to do or stop doing, your brain kicks into gear and will send you messages to remind you what you want to do. This is exactly what happened with those men and women who were in the domestic violence class. Planting the thought "I do not want to go to jail" into their conscious thinking, reminded them not to act out violently the next time they became angry. When a person makes a conscious effort to replace old thinking, they will find new thoughts coming into their consciousness replacing the old thoughts. This is like putting a sticky note on your brain to remind you what you want to change.

Even though we did not discuss this in the last chapter, conscious thinking is needed for incorporating yoga breathing into your life. As you plant the need to breathe into your conscious thought, your brain will remind you to stop and breathe when you begin to react. Each time you respond by breathing, you are building and reinforcing a new neural pathway in your brain. This helps to reinforce the new behavior.

There are three times you can catch yourself when you are working on changing behavior. The first one may sound strange. It is to catch yourself after you have done the deed. Believe it or not, this is actually a way of making progress. In the past, you never paid much attention to your bad behavior. Now, you become aware that you just did something you want to stop. This is not failure, it is progress. Tell yourself "good job" every time you become aware of doing something you want to stop. Then tell yourself you are going to do a better job the next time.

The next way is to catch yourself in the act of doing what you are trying to stop. You are now in the middle of a behavior you have decided to stop, like arguing with your spouse, when you become aware you are arguing. When this happens stop immediately. Tell your spouse you are working on changing your behavior of arguing and need to take a break. Train yourself to stop, and then choose to walk away. If you are in a place where you can do yoga breathing, start. Once you are back in control, redirect your behavior to something positive and more productive. If you need to apologize to your coworker or spouse, then go do it. Apologizing will help to reinforce your positive changes moving forward.

*Take Control of Your Life*

The final step is to stop the behavior before it happens, while it is still a thought. When you become aware you are having a thought to act out, stop, and then tell yourself that you are not going to act this way. Tell yourself you have the ability to control your behavior. Tell yourself whatever is needed to stop the thought from becoming a behavior. The final step takes conscious awareness of your thinking at the moment before you act.

All three responses in an emotional reaction, emotions, behavior, and thinking, can be worked on at the same time or individually

My dad was a heavy, two-pack-a-day smoker for thirty-plus years. One day, he was told by a doctor during a hospital stay that if he did not quit smoking, he would develop emphysema. My dad made a choice at that moment to stop smoking immediately. He never touched another cigarette after that day. Before he changed the behavior, his thinking about smoking had to change, here is what is going to happen to you. This was similar to how those in the domestic violence group changed their behavior.

He replaced smoking with chewing gum. When the urge to smoke came, he would start chewing. Gum wrappers were all over the house. And he chewed gum for about nine months until the urge to smoke was finally gone. He replaced his old behavior of smoking, with new behavior, chewing gum, helping him extinguish the smoking behavior. Learning how to fill the void created when an old behavior stops is important.

My dad became aware he had a problem. He was aware of the future consequences if he continued this behavior. He took the time to weigh his choices, keep smoking and develop terrible lung disease, or quit smoking and prolong his life. He then made a choice to stop the negative behavior. This was followed by replacing the old behavior with new and positive behavior. His life improved as a result and he avoided a very terrible lung disease that could have taken over his life if he had continued smoking.

Life is full of choices that can go in two very opposite directions.

# The Golden Key to Change

*"Whether you think you can, or you think you can't, you're right."*
-Henry Ford

Mr. Ford had it right. Your thinking determines your outlook in life. I would add that if you think you can't, change your mind and think you can. Your thinking has a lot to do with whether you will be successful.

## Changing Your Thinking

Thinking plays a fundamental role in what you feel and why you behave the way you do. Thinking is clearly behind emotional reactions, although it may be hard to see at first. Thinking is behind our behavior.

Standing in line waiting for a turn at a cash register can quickly turn into irritation when you become aware all the other lanes around you are moving faster than you are. Your irritation, which was not there seconds ago, is caused by a thought about the other lanes moving faster. How fast the lanes were moving while standing in line did not create the emotion. The way you think about it did.

The other lines moving faster became the stimulus that created the thought.

Thinking is behind how you behave. This includes the immediate behavior of an emotional reaction, like yelling or cussing when you get angry. Thinking precedes problem behavior that is not connected to an emotion, like drug or alcohol abuse.

Learning a new positive behavior started when you began to implement yoga breathing in your life to control your emotions. Yoga breathing taught you that you had the power to control what you were feeling, the physiological reaction. Applying yoga breathing to your life will be a choice going forward. You choose what you do with this new information.

Thinking is deeply engrained in the type of person you are. Thinking precedes everything you do. Thinking is the golden key to making changes and improving your life.

Thinking stands alone as the main ingredient, but not the only ingredient in change. Thinking gives you the ability to override an emotional reaction and stop problem behavior in its tracks. Changing your thinking must occur before any real change can take place in your life.

Thinking can be seen in the little things of life, like what am I going to eat this morning, and the big things, like buying a home or getting married. However, the importance of thinking is seen in what you spend your time thinking about.

## Thinking-Choices-Behavior-Consequences

I taught anger and stress management as well as corrective thinking classes for probation youth for many years. At the top of my whiteboard in the classroom were the words *thinking, choices, behavior,* and *consequences.* I began the first class by explaining that we never, ever, at any time, stop thinking. The brain is always at work if you are alive.

Although youth may tell me they "weren't thinking" when they committed a crime, I assure them that they were thinking. However, they were not thinking about doing the right thing or the consequences of what could happen if they got caught. They were not thinking about the problems their behavior causes others.

They were thinking about committing a crime and satisfying some personal need, and most of them were thinking they would get away with it. I walk them through how thinking leads to choices, choices to behavior, and behavior to consequences.

The problem in many people's thinking, adolescents and adults alike, is that their thinking is not a complete process. Their thinking at times is not connected to an end result, What If? Very few of the adolescents I worked with spent time thinking about the consequences before they choose to act. This is the fundamental reason for a majority of the problems that you and I create for ourselves—not thinking things through to an end result.

Many decisions people make each day are based on what they want right now. To break this tendency there must be an awareness of what could happen later. Taking the time to weigh the potential consequences will lead to making wiser decisions, and result in having fewer problems. I want to share an example of how thinking things through to an end result can change a person's behavior.

Bob was attending my Corrective Thinking classes at the Youth Camp Halfway House when his probation officer came to me and asked if I would talk with him. If Bob did not make some changes in his current behavior, his probation was going to be violated. This would result in him being arrested and sent to the state juvenile correctional facility in Elko, NV, for nine months. Bob had already spent six months at the Youth Camp, and now three months at a halfway house.

His probation officer stated that Bob's problem was that while he was on house arrest, and on weekend leave, he would sneak out of his house at night after everyone went to bed. He wanted to get out of his house so he could party and smoke marijuana with his friends.

*Take Control of Your Life*

When I sat down with Bob, I asked him what his routine was at night prior to sneaking out of his home. He said that when he was in his bed, he would be picturing his friends partying, smoking pot, drinking, and hanging out with girls. As he pictured this, he felt a powerful urge to get out of bed, leave home, and be with his friends. He admitted he struggled a little with this because he did not want to go to the state correctional facility, but he was having trouble stopping himself. Sound familiar for any behavior you might be struggling with

"I said to him, when you are at home this weekend, I want you to go through the same routine you just told me when you go to bed. I want you to think about your friends and smoking pot, and all the things that go with it."

"I want you to picture yourself sneaking out of your house and going to your friends. Suddenly there is a knock on the door, it is the police. The police enter the house and find you and your friends using drugs and drinking alcohol. The police arrest you and your friends. They load you into one of their police cars and take you to juvenile detention. From there you are placed into a detention cell where you spend the rest of your weekend."

"The juvenile booking center calls the halfway house to tell them you have just been arrested and detained. On Monday, picture yourself in court standing in front of the judge with your probation officer standing next to you. I want you to see yourself explaining to the Judge why you keep sneaking out of your house to party and use drugs. I want you to hear the judge say to you that you are guilty of violating probation and sentence you to Elko. Picture yourself sitting in detention for the next several days waiting to be transported to Elko where you will spend the next nine months."

"Can you do this?" I asked. He said he would.

When I returned to the corrective thinking group the following week, he was there ready for the group. I asked him how his weekend went. He jokingly said that I had ruined his weekend. In other words, visualizing all the consequences that could happen to him if he snuck out of his house had interrupted his fantasy thinking about going to the party. By adding the end result to his fantasy thinking he chose to stay home. He continued to control himself each weekend for the next six weeks until he was successfully released from the halfway house.

The reason I walked him through the weekend scenario was so he could visualize each consequence as it would have happened. If you were to visualize each consequence of what could happen to you before you make a choice to behave in a certain way, would you choose differently?

Corrective thinking helps people to correct the thinking that leads to problem behavior and out-of-control emotions. It teaches the importance of connecting behavior to an end result.

This example shows how Bob's behavior resulted from what he spent his time thinking about, the party, and everything that went with it. Having Bob visualize his fantasy thinking all the way through to the consequences helped him make a better choice, changed his behavior, and his life.

## Cognitive Behavior Therapy

William James, 1842-1910, is considered to be the father of psychology. Long ago, Dr. James said, *"The greatest weapon against stress is man's ability to choose one thought over another."* Dr. James believed that each person has the power to choose between two conflicting thoughts. Dr. James was the forerunner, in my opinion, of Cognitive Behavior Therapy (CBT).

However, Arron Beck, MD, is credited with developing cognitive therapy in the 1960s. Cognitive therapy later morphed into CBT. CBT focuses on how a person's thinking contributes to the problems in their lives and how to develop new ways of thinking to overcome those problems.

Bob's story shows how he was able to choose one thought over another thought. In doing so he was able to make a better choice for his life. Bob was not fighting against stress, but he was fighting temptation, doing something he really wanted to do that would get him in trouble.

It is important you realize you have the ability to choose between two or more competing thoughts. You are not stuck with only one choice at any given time.

A lot of people act on the first thought that comes into their head. Taking the time to have a second thought will result in having more than one choice. Realizing you have more than one choice can help you to avoid the problems that result from bad choices.

The problem most of my probation kids had was they got stuck on the first thought that came to them, and then acted on it. There was no second thought, much less a third, or fourth. Learning to take the time to have a second or third thought can improve your life dramatically.

## Breaking Down Thinking

### Thinking Errors

Stanton Samenow, PhD, has worked within the adult and juvenile criminal justice system for 30+ years. His work with adult criminals resulted in the concept of thinking errors. Thinking errors are a way of thinking that allows a person to break the law with little or no regard for the consequences of their behavior, or the impact their behavior has on others. Treatment is focused on helping people identify their thinking errors that have led to drug addiction, multiple arrests, and prison, sometimes multiple times.

Once a person is able to identify their thinking errors, they focus on replacing these errors with new, non-criminal, and more productive ways of thinking. Let me give you an example of a thinking error that comes from the Commitment to Change video series featuring Dr. Samenow, *I Want It Fast and Easy*. (3)

This thinking error leads to crimes of petty larceny, shoplifting, robbery, burglary, home invasion, and selling drugs. Criminals who want it fast and easy would rather commit these types of crimes than get a job and earn the money they need to buy the things they want. To correct this type of thinking and behavior, the kids in my class needed to look at their thinking to change their behavior.

I would give them a homework assignment to complete before the next class. The assignment was to do one act of random kindness to a stranger. The following week, the kids were to report back what happened.

One youth shared how he was sitting next to a lady on the bus who had dropped her iPhone on the seat when she got up to leave. *Before I proceed, the probation center was located in an impoverished neighborhood.* When he saw the iPhone, he yelled at the lady before she stepped off the bus. "Wait, I have your iPhone," he said. When she was handed the iPhone, she told him a grateful "thank you."

In doing a random act of kindness, each youth was to be aware of what the person said or did that had received the act of kindness. They were to be aware of how it made them feel when they did something kind for someone else. To this question, he replied that giving the iPhone to the person, "made me feel really good inside."

How you feel when you do something kind for someone else is lost when you become self-centered, selfish, and out for yourself. We lose sight of how good it feels to do the right thing for another person. How we treat others is entrenched in our worldview and how we think about ourselves. By doing one act of kindness, this young man's thinking about himself and others was changed, at least temporarily. My hope is that he can see the good that resides in him and continue to make changes in his life.

After he told the story, I asked him what he would have done if he had not been given the assignment to do a random act of kindness that week. He said he would have kept the iPhone. I also had kids who returned wallets with the money in it, helped elderly women put their groceries in their car, and bought food for or gave money to a homeless person. See how planting a new thought into these young men and women's thinking caused them to behave differently.

The thought of doing a random act of kindness had been placed in the back of their mind waiting for an opportunity to happen. This is how the brain works. Once the opportunity presented itself, this young man's brain kicked into gear and reminded him that he needed to fulfill the homework assignment.

Future thinking in my adolescent delinquents was lost on the concept of future consequences. Like my adolescent friend at the halfway house, once he was able to add the thought of consequences to his thinking, he was able to make better choices. My adolescent friend on the bus was able to think about someone else. This happened because a thought had been planted into their thinking days earlier. These adolescents acted differently than they would have because of new thinking. New thinking leads to new choices, which leads to new behavior. If this young man's thinking had remained the same, as he said, "I would have kept the iPhone."

Another problem with criminal thinking is that there is little thought given to how their behavior harms others. The thinking error, *"no one was harmed,"* is addressed in the Commitment to Change video series. (4). A criminal does not consider the pain or suffering his victims go through before acting. The criminal's way of thinking is if there is no blood, or the person did not have to go to the hospital, then no harm, no foul. Many criminals only think of harm in terms of serious physical harm or blood spilt.

The criminal does not think about the harm he causes the victim in terms of property loss. They think they can replace what was taken from them because the insurance company will repay it. They do not comprehend the emotional harm a person suffers that comes with having a gun pointed at them or the financial harm that comes by stealing a car or breaking into a person's home. They do not think of the harm it causes their family when they get arrested or end up in a detention facility. When you are not aware of the harm you cause others by your bad behavior, then you will end up hurting a lot of people as you go through life.

One day, I was thinking about this thinking error when I realized that we all have the potential to develop our own personal thinking errors at times separate from criminal behavior. When you and I lose sight of treating people with respect and kindness anything can happen. The spouse who commits adultery does not think about the harm it will cause their spouse or their children. Will they be arrested for adultery? Not in the USA. But the harm that is caused by the betrayal that comes with adultery can be devastating. What about the harm that is caused by lying to or stealing from someone you know, especially when it is family?

People today do not give much thought to how divorce can harm their children. The adolescents I have worked with talk about the emotional pain they have suffered caused by their parent's divorce. Emotional harm results when we are not sensitive to how we talk to and around our children, or how we treat others.

I want it fast and easy can lead to non-criminal problem behaviors like gambling, credit card debt, and investing money in get-rich-quick schemes. Whether it is criminal behavior or irresponsible behavior, it all begins with how we think.

Changing your thinking means you will need to quit making excuses, or blaming others for your bad choices, behaviors, and the consequences you have suffered.

I want to briefly share with you some other areas you may want to consider changing that are related to thinking.

- Changing negative thoughts into positive ones. Each one of us makes a choice as to whether we will dwell on the negative thoughts and things in life or focus on the positive.
- Changing your bad attitude into a good attitude. The only person that can change your attitude is yourself. If your attitude sucks, so does life. Your thinking creates your

attitude. You are responsible for your attitude, not other people. When your attitude is positive, life is much brighter. It is a choice.
- Changing how you see and think about yourself. The way you think about yourself determines how you feel about yourself. If you do not like what you see, you have the ability to change yourself. For some of you, changing how you think about yourself could bring about a whole new you. In addition, some of the problems you have had in the past will fade away when you change how you see yourself.
- Changing how you see and think about others. Enough said.

Just as a key unlocks a door, thinking unlocks your ability to change. Unfortunately, we can be so focused on the behavior as the problem, we do not realize it is our thinking that is the real problem.

# What Makes Up Our Thinking

*"Thinking is the hardest work there is, which is
probably the reason, so few engage in it."*
-Henry Ford

## Thinking

Most of us do not give much thought to how we think or the effect our thinking has on how we live. Your thinking has led you to where you are at today in your life. Thinking preceded every choice you have made. It does not matter whether you were actively thinking those choices through, or whether you passively made those choices by doing the first thing that came to mind.

This step will be the one that will require the greatest amount of awareness and effort to change. You will need to be actively engaged in the process of changing how you think.

*"We can't solve problems by using the same kind
of thinking we used when we created them."*
-Albert Einstein

## Thoughts

The most basic component of thinking is thought. Your brain is continually on the job. It does not take time off. Hundreds of thousands of thoughts pass through your brain every day. You cannot count them all. Thoughts rapidly pass into and out of your stream of consciousness. Thoughts are here one second, gone the next. Thoughts do not mean that we are thinking, only that our brain is working.

Thoughts are similar to someone turning the dial on a radio to find a particular station they want to listen to. As they turn the dial, they pass over various other stations where they hear various soundbites like a voice speaking or a note from a song. Eventually, they settle on a station where they can listen to a complete song, the news, or a sporting event.

Thoughts are like turning a dial in your brain trying to find a station to stop and listen to. Some thoughts that pass through your mind are meaningless, and some are just plain crazy. There are thoughts that you would never want another person to know you have. Thoughts come and go at a high rate of speed. The thought you had seconds ago moves on to a new and different thought.

The thing about thoughts is you decide what thought you want to stop and spend time thinking about. You choose. You are not forced to think about one thing over another. You choose. No one tells you what to think about. The fact that you chose what thought you are going to spend time thinking about is important with regard to learning how to change your thinking.

Thoughts can be internally generated, as seen in what we say to ourselves in the morning getting out of bed. Thoughts can be externally generated by what is going on around us, or by what someone says to us. A quick example of this is two friends sitting together having a conversation when one of them asks the other; "do you want to get something to eat?" You were not thinking about eating before they asked the question, but now you are thinking about it. Your thought about eating was created by what someone said. Whether thoughts are internally or externally created does not matter. Thoughts are only thoughts until you spend time thinking about them.

The first line of thinking is your thoughts. You get to decide which ones you are going to spend time thinking about. You determine whether you will focus on positive or negative thoughts.

A female I know was talking about how her brothers and sisters tease her because she is thin, which makes her angry. My friend works out regularly, eats right, and stays fit. When they make fun, she reacts based on how she thinks about what they are saying, which is, why are they are making fun of me. This creates a negative reaction in her based on how she thinks about what they are saying.

I said to my friend, turn the thought that "they are making fun of you" into a compliment "for being fit." Just say to them thanks for noticing. I work hard at staying in shape and appreciate when others recognize the result. It really does not matter why she thinks they are making fun of her, what matters is how she thinks about what they are saying. She has the ability to decide whether she wants to take a positive or negative approach.

A couple of weeks later when she was at the gym, I asked how she was doing with changing her brother's and sister's comments into compliments. She said it was going very well. She was no longer reacting by getting upset at them anymore. In fact, her siblings were surprised that she had quit reacting to their teasing. She was able to make the change in her thinking by replacing the negative thoughts with a new and positive way of thinking about what they were saying. This is the key to changing your emotional reactions; change how you think about what people are doing or saying.

The first area to look at in changing your thinking is the thought you choose to spend your time thinking about, as well as how you choose to think about what others do or say to you.

## Beliefs

The second component of thinking is beliefs. A belief is something you hold to be true. Beliefs are fundamental to how you live and the choices you make every day. Beliefs work at a non-conscious level most of the time, meaning you are not consciously thinking about what you believe when you make a choice to do something.

Our beliefs are formed by experiences, education, what others tell us, and what we see, hear, and read. New beliefs are continually being formed while old beliefs can change. Beliefs can be static meaning they may never change, such as a deep-seated belief in God. They can be dynamic, meaning they can change at any time. Beliefs play a big part in how you think, make decisions, and behave.

For instance, if you believe hard work will pay off in the end, you will continue to work hard even when the end result has not happened yet. On the other hand, if you believe you are entitled to certain things in life, like a job promotion, you may not put in an effort to make it happen. Entitlement thinking is running rampant today. It rests on what you believe.

Beliefs can be profound or trivial. Beliefs cover big things, small things, and things that do not really matter like what sports team is better than another. Beliefs determine what we believe we can and cannot do. They affect how we see ourselves and how we see other people. Beliefs are interwoven throughout our daily activities.

I just recently drove across town on a Saturday to buy a part I needed to fix my backyard gate. When I got there, they were closed. I made the drive believing the store would be open, but my belief did not make it happen. Because we believe something to be true, does not make it true.

Beliefs can change. Maybe I should have called before I drove across town. I am sure some of you may have done a similar thing and did not call before you made the trip. My belief about this store being open on a Saturday changed after my experience. This is a type of dynamic, changeable belief.

You are probably sitting in a chair while you are reading this. When you sat down, did you believe the chair would hold you up? Sure, you did. But were you consciously thinking about it holding you up when you sat down? Have you ever sat in a chair that broke?

You believe the brakes in your car will work every time you get in your car to drive. But brakes can fail. We make many of these types of decisions every day based on a subconscious set of beliefs.

Many of the probation kids I worked with believed they would not get caught. They were immune. The consequences of this mistaken belief cost them their freedom. Until they can change their belief, "I won't get caught," they will continue to risk losing their freedom. This particular belief guides the choices many of these adolescents make every day. The opposite belief is also true too. If you believe you could get caught, you are less likely to do it.

A belief can affect your future in a positive or negative way. Some of the adolescents I worked with believed that school was a waste of time, so they dropped out. Imagine their surprise when they find out that it will be difficult to find a good-paying job because they quit school. Their limited belief in the present moment, school is a waste of time, will affect their lives further than they can see down the road.

Beliefs play a role in your choices, your behavior, and what you think about yourself and others. Beliefs are behind how you choose to live. I had two friends who were brothers that died in their forty's due to cirrhosis of the liver from drinking hard alcohol. I do not think they believed that drinking would kill them in their forty's. If they had known what was coming in the future, would they have changed their behavior and their thinking about alcohol?

Here are some questions to ask yourself to check your beliefs:

- Are your beliefs grounded in reality? Have you heard of the Flat World Society? You can imagine what they believe.

New information is probably not going to change their thinking about the shape of the earth, or about sailing around the world. It is foolish to make choices in life that are not grounded in reality. New information can correct faulty beliefs.

- Are your beliefs realistic, meaning under normal circumstances could these things happen? If you believe something can happen in reality, then you need to put all your effort into making it happen. If your belief is not realistic, get rid of it.
- Does your belief put the responsibility for doing something on yourself or on someone else to it do for you? For instance, do you believe it is the responsibility of your spouse to make you happy? Any belief that puts the responsibility on another person to make something happen in their life is unrealistic.
- Are your beliefs distorted by your past experiences? This does not always happen, but more often than naught, it does. A person's past experience can affect a person's thinking and behavior in the present time. A person whose parents divorced when they were young, may decide that they are not going to get married to this wonderful person because they want to avoid what happened to their parents. The person's choice and behavior about marriage are based on a belief this could happen to them. No one can predict the future outcome of something before it happens. Reexamine whether any of your decisions have been made based on predicting what you think might happen.

  Being hurt in a past relationship does not mean it will happen in the next relationship. But if you do make a decision about relationships based on a previous experience, you may miss finding your dream person. However, there is always a risk in making certain life decisions. To overcome unfounded or distorted beliefs, as well as the fears that can come with them, means you have to be willing to challenge any belief that is distorted by past experiences and failures.

- Are your beliefs correct? We tend to believe what we believe. What I mean by this is we tend not to question our beliefs. Most people believe what they have been taught by authority figures, teachers, and parents. We tend to believe things we read in the newspaper or hear on the news. We believe what we believe, that is until we are challenged by others to question it for ourselves. Cigarette smoking was not seriously considered a health risk when I was growing up. That belief has changed. You may believe the world should be fair, but guess what, it is not. If that is what you choose to believe, be prepared to be disappointed. You need to be able to check your beliefs to see if they need to be replaced or updated by new information.

- Do you believe what people tell you without checking it out? There are kids I have talked to who have beaten up other kids because their friends told them a person was bad-mouthing them. One kid I interviewed never checked this information out for himself to see if it was true. Unfortunately, he was in juvenile detention for attacking an innocent person because his friends had lied to him. The kid who this boy attacked had done nothing wrong. Have you ever believed something a friend had told you that turned out to be false? Simply put, because someone says so, does not make it so. A big mistake can be made when you do not fact-check things out for yourself to see if they are true.

- Are your beliefs accurate? I remember buying something on eBay and when it arrived it was not what I thought I had bought. Needless to say, I was not happy. When I went back and took the time to read the description of the product, I found I had misread the description for what I was buying. It was my mistake. My belief in what I thought I was buying was not accurate.

- Beliefs can limit what you do in life? If you believe you cannot do something, you probably will not attempt to do it. This is called a self-limiting belief. This type of belief is created by how you think about yourself. The good news is that you can change your self-concept by taking the time to change what you believe about yourself.

  For many years in the world of track and field, it was believed that no person would ever be able to run a mile under four minutes. Then in 1954, a runner broke the four-minute mile at three minutes and fifty-nine seconds. Since 1954, there have been numerous runners who have run the mile under four minutes. Once the belief that a mile could not be run under four minutes was broken, it opened the door for many people to believe they could also do it. Self-limiting beliefs are harmful. They can keep you from following your dreams and desires.

- Do your beliefs affect how you see others? Absolutely. Have you ever been told by another person that so and so was not a very good person, and as a result, you formed a negative opinion about them? Later, when you got to know that person, you found out that what you had believed about them was not true. New information you received from being around that person changed what you believed about them. Changing a belief can go a long way in helping you make changes in your life, but it takes new information.

## Perception

Perception is how you interpret what you see, hear, or experience. Perception is not necessarily what did happen; it is how you think about what happened. Take going to a movie as an example of perception. Two people experience the same movie. When the movie is over one person likes it, while the other does not. Who is right?

Both are. A person's perception determines whether they like the movie or not. The movie is reality. Perception is how you interpret the reality of what you just saw.

My sister and I have different perceptions about growing up in our family. Our perceptions are probably not based one hundred percent on reality. Now that we are older, are our memories really accurate about everything that happened in our family fifty years ago? Probably not. The things that happened to us growing up affect the way we see and feel about our family in the present.

We may have had similar experiences at times growing up, but we can interpret them differently. We have had different experiences that affect how we see our family. Being seven years apart in age can also play a part in our perceptions. The problem comes when perceptions are not based in reality because a person's perception can become their reality, and not accurate.

This is where perception becomes tricky. If I believe something is true based on my perception of what I experienced, then it becomes hard to convince me that I am wrong. I may believe that I saw a flying saucer last night. Even when I am presented with facts that contradict what I thought I saw I may still disagree.

One way to look at reality versus perception is magic. Magic—specifically, illusions—can cause us to believe something to be true that is not. Separating reality from perception in an illusion is like separating what you think you saw, from what actually happened.

I have seen Penn and Teller at the Rio Hotel on occasion. A certain illusion caused the audience to believe something had happened magically, that really did not happen magically. After completing the illusion, Penn and Teller took the same illusion, pulled back the curtains, and acted it out. This time the audience saw how the illusion actually worked in real-time to produce the result we had seen. The end result of what we thought had happened, and the end result of how it actually happened was the same. But what took place in real-time was different from what we thought had happened. One was reality; the other was our perception of reality.

Take a situation where two boys grow up in the same home. In this home, the father is an alcoholic and abusive. The two boys grow up into adulthood. One becomes a substance abuser with a failed marriage, barely making it in life. His brother becomes a successful businessman with a stable marriage and family. When each man is asked how they got to where they are in life, both of them respond it was what they learned from their father. Each brother's perspective of what they learned growing up in their family was very different and it showed in how it played out in their life.

In real life, you have the brothers Whitey and William Bulger. Whitey was an Irish gangster and former hitman who ruled the Irish underworld for a period of time in Boston. His brother was highly educated and was president of the Massachusetts State Senate for eighteen years. These brothers grew up under the same roof, but their paths after they left home ended at opposite ends of the spectrum of life.

Perceptions are difficult to change because we tend to believe our perceptions are accurate. They are not always accurate. Take two people who witness the same incident and then are asked to tell what happened. Even when they are completely honest about what they saw, their stories will not match every detail. Mixed in with the facts of what happened are their personal perceptions of what they saw and think happened. This can lead to variations in their stories.

Check your perceptions to see if they are accurate or faulty. If they are not accurate, change them.

## Self-Talk

Self-talk can be one of the most problematic areas in the way a person thinks and behaves. This area of thinking is in the greatest need of change in most people. Self-talk can be both positive and negative. It is the negative self-talk that needs to change.

Self-talk is the conversation you have with yourself in your head. These conversations are more than just thoughts passing through. Self-talk is a back and forth of thoughts done as if you are having a conversation with yourself.

Self-talk is usually focused on a specific line of thought. It can occur in the middle of something that is happening to you, or moments after a situation has happened to you. Self-talk determines what you are going to do or not do, what you will say or not say in reacting. Negative self-talk can escalate your emotions and turn a minor situation into a major one needlessly. Positive self-talk can slow you down, help you think so you can make a good decision.

Self-talk goes like this with the kids I worked with. Someone says something they do not like, then a conversation starts in their head. "Did you hear what they said to me?" "Am I going to let them get away with that?" "Nobody can talk to me like that." "What am I going do about it?" And on and on, ad nauseam.

As this conversation goes on, their emotions escalate. They may now be preparing to cut loose on someone. These conversations only take seconds but can last longer.

Positive self-talk could keep you from acting out and making the situation worse. Self-talk, in and of itself, is neither good nor bad; it is how you use it. Negative self-talk escalates your emotions and increases the likelihood of acting out. Positive self-talk can calm you down and help you make better decisions, keeping you from doing something foolish.

Self-talk includes how you talk about yourself. This type of negative self-talk is about how you see and think about yourself, your self-worth, self-esteem, and self-confidence.

People can tell themselves they are not attractive, stupid, fat, no one likes them, and on and on. You do not need anyone to tell you these things, you can tell these things to yourself. This type of self-talk is connected to the beliefs you have about yourself and your abilities. Many of the things you believe about yourself began in childhood.

An example of negative self-talk is when you tell yourself that you cannot do something, even when you are fully capable of doing it. This results in not even trying to do certain things. The limiting beliefs you have about yourself will need to be challenged if you want to move forward and achieve success in life.

To change negative self-talk, you will need to catch yourself when you are doing it. Self-awareness will be needed. Once you have identified the negative self-talk, you will need to replace it with positive self-talk. Stopping negative self-talk is not enough. You must replace it with positive self-talk. "I can't do that" is replaced with "I can do it." Changing self-talk takes time and practice but brings great rewards.

Self-talk is similar to rumination. Self-talk focuses on how you talk to yourself when you are in specific situations. Rumination is the intentional playing of a situation over and over for a period of time after it is over. Rumination can go on for days or weeks at a time, while self-talk is focused more on the present moment and what you are feeling. Rumination is generally focused on a grievance that someone has regarding something that happened to them. They feel a need to resolve the grievance, so they play it over and over in their head until they come up with a solution or decide to let it go. Sometimes, they can resolve it peaceably, other times, maybe not.

Negative self-talk and rumination contribute to keeping our emotions turned on for much longer than they need to be. By learning how to change self-talk and stop rumination, you will find you have a greater ability to walk away from situations and make better choices. Stopping ruminations and negative self-talk can have a big impact on making changes in your life.

## Expectations

An expectation is defined as something you think or believe should happen. When the outcome is not what you expected to happen, be prepared for an emotional reaction. There is nothing wrong with having expectations. The problem with expectations generally arises when the expectation is unspoken.

If an expectation involves another person, then it should be spoken and agreed upon by both parties. Expectations are typically laid out in a job. When you are applying for a job, you should know what the job responsibilities are, the days and hours you work, your salary and benefits, as well as lesser areas like dress code before you accept the position. There may be some surprises later, but the majority of expectations are laid out in plain sight. This helps a person know what is expected of them if they decide to take the job. The last thing you want would be a surprise. Unfortunately, expectations in relationships are not always spoken aloud and can come as a surprise to the other person.

Expectations need to be realistic. When they are not, failed expectations can lead to negative emotions like disappointment or discouragement. You expect to get a good grade or a job you applied for, and if it does not happen, how do you react?

Was your expectation realistic? Did you study to get a good grade? Were you qualified for the job you applied for? If not, then the expectation was not grounded in reality. If you did not do what you needed to do to get a good grade, or you were unqualified for the position you applied for, then your expectation was not based on reality.

If the expectation you have is realistic and attainable and you fall short, you can always regroup and start over. I remember talking with the president of a successful home-building corporation who was concerned that a pending divorce could affect the future of his company. I asked how he would deal with it if that happened. He quickly responded by saying that he had accomplished success before, and if he had to, he could do it all over again. Although he did not want to have to do that, his expectation that he could rebuild was realistic. It was based on his past history of success and experience.

Failed personal expectations do not mean you give up. You must keep your thinking in balance. If your expectation is realistic and attainable then go for it. If not, then make some changes to make it realistic and try again.

The biggest problem with expectations is that they are not always out in the open. For many of us, it is only after expectations are not met that we become aware they were there. Make no mistake about it, expectations play a big part in relationships, whether spoken or unspoken. Put your expectations out in the open for people to see in your relationships. When you do this both parties understand what is required of them. Now each person can make an informed decision. This should result in greater relationship satisfaction.

One couple I counseled with had a different set of expectations that was causing them problems. The female had an expectation that in an intimate relationship people should share certain personal things with their partner. Everything needed to be out in the open. This lady was very open about her feelings and in expressing personal things going on in her life. Her expectation was that her companion needed to reciprocate by being more open about his feelings and personal aspects of his life. Many women feel this way in intimate relationships. When these expectations are not met it generally leads to relationship problems. The issue here is that the other person in a relationship can have a different set of beliefs and expectations about sharing personal information. Gender and cultural differences, as well as the family you grew up in all play a part in how people behave, relate, and express their expectations in a relationship.

This woman believed her expectations were reasonable and therefore should happen. It is not unusual for a person to believe their perspective is the right one and that the other person is wrong. The inability of the other person to accept how their partner sees things differently leads to feelings of frustration and dissatisfaction in relationships.

I said to the woman that having different views about sharing personal information in a relationship is not about who is right or who is wrong, it is about having different expectations and being able to accept those differences. Once you can do this, you can negotiate through your differences.

# A Biblical Perspective on Thinking

*"Come now, and let us reason together," says
the Lord, "Though your sins are like scarlet,
they shall be white as snow; Though they are
red like crimson, they shall be as wool."*
(Isaiah 1:18)

## John the Baptist

All four New Testament gospel accounts mention John the Baptizer. John is a unique character who bursts onto the pages of the New Testament. Prior to his appearing four hundred years have passed between the last book of the Old Testament, Malachi, and John's appearance in the Gospel of Matthew. Those four hundred years are referred to as God's silent period.

John is a transitional person living between the end of the Old Testament and the beginning of the New Testament. He is considered an Old Testament prophet living in New Testament times. His job responsibilities were to proclaim the arrival of the Messiah and the coming of the kingdom of God. His message emphasized a need to repent, followed by water baptism.

What we want to look at is what the Bible has to say about our thinking.

There are three scriptures in Matthew that reference the word repent or repentance.

- "… Repent for the kingdom of heaven is at hand." (Matthew 3:2.) John has been sent by God to prepare the way for the coming Messiah and the arrival of the kingdom of God. Repentance prepares the hearts of the people to receive the Messiah when He comes.
- "Therefore, bring forth fruit worthy of repentance," (Matthew 3:8.) John's message identifies true repentance by a change in behavior, which John calls fruit.
- "I indeed baptize you with water unto repentance …" (Matthew 3:11.) Water baptism is the outward evidence a person has believed John's message and repented.

Repentance is usually defined as turning your life around, going in the opposite direction, or a 180-degree change. The problem with this definition is because it puts the focus on the end result of repentance, a behavior change. It misses addressing what precipitated the change. It is not that this explanation is wrong per se; the focus is limited and misses the full picture. The word that has been translated into English as repentance is the word for thinking in the Greek language.

## Repentance and Thinking

The Greek word for repentance is metanoia. The word metanoia is made up of two Greek words, *meta* and *noeo*. The first word to look at is noeo, which is a verb. It is defined

- To perceive with the mind, to understand.
- To think upon, heed, ponder, and consider.

The word noeo refers to thinking, not to behavior. Noeo as a verb identifies a specific action that takes place, to think.

The second word meta is a preposition that means after. When you combine these two words, they form metanoia, which means *"after thinking,"* or *"to think after."* Metanoia implies an action takes place after thinking about something that has occurred. In repentance, it is a thinking change that precedes a change in behavior, the result.

Thinking is the process by which we make decisions about what we believe, how we behave and live our lives. John is challenging the people to *change their thinking* about how they are living. This change in thinking is to be reflected in a change of behavior, fruit. Thinking is the process; behavior change is the fruit.

## The Fruit of Repentance

John's preaching to the people comes with a warning. "… every tree that does not bear good fruit is cut down and thrown into the fire." (Luke 3:9.) The people John is speaking to recognize John as a prophet. Old Testament prophets who were sent by God prophesied of judgment if the people did not repent of their sins and turn back to God.

They understood that John's words were a warning to them and that they needed to be careful about how they would respond to his message. Their concern leads to, "So the people asked him, saying, what shall we do then?" (Luke 3:10.)

John gives three distinct answers to this question to three different groups of people who are in his audience. Summarizing their question, if I were to repent, what would that look like for me.

- The first group is the common people like you and me. "He answered and said to them, He who has two tunics, let him give to him who has none; and he who has food, let him do likewise." (Luke 3:11.) Behavior change for them is to be reflected in their treatment of other people, especially the poor. If they have the ability to give something to someone who is in need, they are to give it and not withhold it. John's reply is a practical one. It addresses how we as Christians are to look at, think about, and treat people. A change in their thinking would result in a change in how they responded to other people and their needs. The fruit of repentance will be seen in caring for and giving to others.

- The second group was tax collectors. "And he said to them, collect no more than what is appointed to you." (Luke 3:12-13.) The tax collectors were usually Jewish people who were appointed by the Romans to collect taxes from the Jewish people. Tax collectors were notorious for cheating people by overcharging them more than they owed. Doing this allowed them to fill their pockets and raise their standard of living. Many of them were dishonest and used their position of authority to abuse people. For this reason, tax collectors were despised by the average person of their day. The fruit of repentance for the tax collector was to be seen in being honest, quit overcharging people, and be fair. They were to treat all people fairly in their duties as a tax collector.

- The third group was soldiers. "Likewise, the soldiers asked him, saying, and what shall we do? So he said to them, do not intimidate anyone or accuse falsely, and be content with your wages." (Luke 3:14.) Soldiers could easily abuse their authority by making unfair demands on people who were unable to do anything about how they were being treated. The soldiers could falsely charge a person with a crime and then bribe them to make the accusations go away. The fruit of repentance for the soldier is to quit using their authority to take advantage of people, do not let greed cause you to take from others what is not yours to take, and treat all people fairly and with respect.

The fruit of repentance in all three groups is zeroed in on how we are to treat people. John's response hits at the heart of true change. The change in our thinking should result in a change of behavior that can be seen by others, and in how we treat others.

There is nothing in this text that identifies repentance as an emotional response. Repentance may come with an emotional response, but it is not a requirement. Repentance is not about feeling; it is about changing thinking, making different choices, which then changes behavior. There may be times in your life when repentance may cause a strong emotional feeling, but if it does not lead to behavior change, then it is not repentance and therefore meaningless.

## Thinking and Change

"And do not be conformed to this world, but be transformed by the renewing of your mind, that you may prove what is that good and acceptable and perfect will of God." (Romans 12:2.)

We need to look at some Greek words used in this New King James text beginning with conformed. The Greek word is *schema*, which in English is the word we use for a schematic. A schematic is a type of diagram of how something looks and/or basic how it works.

Conformity is expressed by an outward appearance of uniformity, the schema as seen as kids dressing, talking, looking, and behaving in similar ways within their identified peer group. It will be seen in uniformity of thought as one wants to fit in and belonging to a group.

It is easy to pick out adolescents who are trying to fit in with what group they want to be a part of. Conformity can also be seen in thinking. This can quickly be seen in political views as defined by a political organization.

The second Greek word is translated transformed in our text. The Greek word is *metamorphoo*. From this word comes our English word metamorphous. Metamorphous is defined as transformation. It is the process of change that takes place in nature as something is turning into something different. Most of us know this word from the transformation of a caterpillar into a butterfly. The transformation into a butterfly begins inward, in the cocoon, followed by an outward manifestation as it breaks free after a struggle.

*Metamorphoo* is made up of two Greek words, *meta*, which we saw in metanoia, followed by the root word *morphoo*, which means changing form in keeping with *inner reality*. Real outward change, it is saying, only takes place as a result of a true inward change—the inward reality—first. The butterfly that breaks out of the cocoon is manifesting what had developed in the cocoon.

Paul is pointing out that the process of transformation begins with the renewing of your mind. A renewed mind brings about a change in your thinking that results in a change in your behavior. Christian transformation is a process of changing how we used to be, by changing how we think.

In Adam's fall, man takes on a sinful nature. The transformation of a Christian is the changing of our sinful inherited nature from Adam into the likeness of Jesus Christ. "Therefore, if anyone is in Christ, he is a new creation; old things have passed away, behold all things have become new." (II Corinthians 5:17.) Becoming new refers to the process of the Christian breaking free from his fleshly cocoon. The new nature is to be a reflection of Jesus Christ in you.

The transformation process is an ongoing work that begins with spiritual birth. John the Apostle refers to spiritual birth as being born of the Spirit (John 3:6) and being born-again (John 3:7). Receiving Jesus into your life produces new birth.

Spiritual birth is the starting point for what Paul refers to when he says that we are a new creation. We have been born again and the process of transformation is ongoing as old behavior and attitudes are replaced with new attitudes and new behavior that reflects Jesus's nature in us. For instance, we probably all could improve on loving our neighbors. The process of transformation is not something you can do yourself. Transformation begins with spiritual birth and continues as the Holy Spirit works in you to bring about the changes in your thinking, emotions, and behavior.

# Thinking and Who We Are

*"A man is what he thinks about all day long."*
-Ralph Waldo Emerson

## Dr. Jekyll and Mr. Hyde

Most people have heard of the story of Dr. Jekyll and Mr. Hyde. What you may not have thought while reading the story or watching the movie is how the story may apply to your life.

Dr. Jekyll is an educated, decent, church-going man. As a doctor, he is compassionate and dedicated to helping others. Dr. Jekyll, being aware of man's dual nature—good and evil—begins an experiment, wanting to separate man's two natures. He develops a serum he hopes will accomplish this and begins by experimenting on animals. But instead of waiting a period of time to see if the animals suffer any adverse side effects, he chooses to use the serum on himself.

The serum creates an alternate personality called Mr. Hyde, an evil personification of Dr. Jekyll's dark side. The difference between these two personalities is highlighted by the contrast between Dr. Jekyll's and Mr. Hyde's physical appearance. The contrast between their personalities is even greater. Mr. Hyde is aggressive, violent, and given over to satisfying his lusts and desires.

The serum transforms Dr. Jekyll into a different person, one who is unrecognizable to his fiancé and friends. As Dr. Jekyll continues to drink the serum, Mr. Hyde grows stronger, while Dr. Jekyll is weakened. As the dark side grows stronger, I will let you read the book or watch the movie to find out what happens.

## Thinking and Its Relation to the Serum

Dr. Jekyll's serum represents what you spend your time thinking about. The person you are, has been shaped by how you think. How you think is the determining factor in building or failing to build character.

How you think is shaped by what you spend your time thinking about. Images and messages, written and spoken words, all influence your thinking. Advertising understands this principle and uses these images to influence what you buy.

Dr. Jekyll's serum causes his negative side to grow stronger. In our case, the serum is the bad thinking that reinforces our out-of-control emotions and behavior.

A powerful image that can influence a person's thinking and effect their behavior is pornography. These images are powerful and can have a greater effect on a person than even advertising does trying to sell their products. Both send powerful images—one to buy, one for sex. Visual images and written and spoken words have an influence on how you think.

Working in juvenile probation I had contact with many adolescents who got involved with pornography. Having access to a computer, along with access to pornography, changed their lives. The sexual images of hardcore pornography became seared into their visual memories. You cannot take an eraser and make them disappear once they are viewed.

After these adolescents viewed these images, they developed a strong desire to experience sex. Most of these kids were socially awkward and had not yet become involved in dating. But now they wanted sex, not a date. Pornography had created a strong sexual desire.

Because they were not in a relationship with another person, they chose to act out on children, many times their siblings. The sexual thoughts and urges caused by these images were not there prior to viewing pornography. For these kids, pornography was Dr. Jekyll's serum. The more they viewed pornography, the stronger the urge for sex became, and the dark side came out. Sexual thoughts infiltrated their thinking continually. We must remember these adolescents did not start out this way, but their thinking had changed after viewing porn.

Drinking Dr. Jekyll's serum can be seen in drug abuse and addiction. I have not met a single person who set out to become an alcoholic or an addict. Drug use usually begins with experimentation. As a person's drug use increases, so does the amount of time they spend thinking about and using drugs. Many of the adolescents I worked with admitted that they had random thoughts about using drugs throughout the day, including while they were sitting in an English or math class.

Prior to getting involved with drugs, they were not struggling with these types of thoughts throughout their day. Just like pornography, the more these adolescents thought about drugs, the more their drug use increased.

Delinquency and criminal behavior are no different. A large number of teenagers engage in some type of delinquent behavior at some point. Most of these teenagers, including the ones I have worked with, will grow up to be good people. Research has shown that most kids outgrow this type of behavior and become productive adults. Unfortunately, there will be some kids whose behavior does not change. These kids will either graduate to the adult system or end up dead. We need to remember that these adolescents did not start out this way, but their thinking led to where they were.

Adult criminals are no different. Most of them started out as regular kids growing up. Criminality usually starts with minor crimes in a similar way drug use begins with experimentation. Once the door has been opened, a person may begin to spend more time thinking about committing other crimes, using drugs, or viewing pornography, than living their life in a positive and productive way. These adolescents and adults did not start out this way.

Mental health issues can start out small and grow to the point where it defines how a person sees themself. I know adults and adolescents who began to identify themselves by their mental health diagnosis and the drugs they take. Ongoing mental health issues can alter a person's personality. But people with mental health problems do not start out that way.

## What You Think and How You Behave Shapes Your Character

Thinking first, followed by behavior, is fundamental to character development, who you are. Dr. Jekyll did not start out as Mr. Hyde. The change was gradual. Similarly, what may have started out as a little peek at porn, experimentation with marijuana, or a minor crime like petty larceny, can slowly take hold of who you are. Over time, the behavior changes you.

Mr. Hyde represents the people who have lost control of their life. Mr. Hyde represents an addiction that has taken control of a person's behavior or criminality that has led to multiple arrests and time in jail. I have heard parents describe this type of change in their kids, "I want my child back," they say. To them, the child in my office is different from the child they have raised.

I have heard a similar thing from the women whose husbands were sitting in the Domestic Violence classes I supervised. The wife might say things like their husband is not really like this, or that he only becomes violent when he is using alcohol or drugs, which is pretty much every night. Most of them say he was not that way when they married him.

## The Doctor's Serum and Mental Health

I have been involved with many people who have suffered from depression, beginning with my family. Ongoing depression can alter a person's personality and behavior.

A common denominator in people who are depressed is in their thinking. People who are depressed tend to focus on the negative things in their life. Depressed people tend not to spend time thinking about how to overcome their problems, or how to get over their depression apart from medication. They can easily fall into the trap of letting the medication take care of the problem while minimizing what they need to do for themselves.

Depression can turn a person inward, leading to self-absorption. This causes depressed people difficulty seeing outside of the box of depression. When this happens it becomes very difficult, but not impossible, to break through their thinking and encourage them that their life can improve. For this reason, professional counseling may be needed to help them to get outside of themselves, find ways they can solve their problems, and improve their life. Anyone who has lived with a family member or friend who has been depressed for a period of time knows that they are not the same person they used to be. Depression has had a negative effect on who they are. Depressed people do not start out as depressed people.

Your thinking shapes your character and determines your behavior. To overcome addictive behavior, stop criminal behavior, and overcome mental health issues means you will have to break the repetitive pattern of thinking that has led to these things shaping you and your repetitive behavior that leads to failing over and over again.

## Character Flaws

I am sure that most of you are not in need of a character overhaul. But you might have a need for a character flaw tune-up.

Flawed thinking generally lies in the background of a person's mind until an opportunity presents itself to reveal the flaw. Even though it is only a flaw, it can lead to negative consequences. The flaw is usually revealed in a situation where a choice has to be made as it relates to right and wrong, or appropriate or inappropriate. I want to share an example I used in my training with probation officers, and with the adolescents in my corrective thinking classes.

You are at the bank cashing your paycheck of one thousand dollars. As you stand there the cashier counts your money back to you. When the cashier is done counting the money, you turn and count your money as you walk away. You find that you have one hundred dollars too much. What do you do?

Most probation kids said they would keep the money. Unfortunately, I had probation officers who said they would keep the money too. The purpose of this exercise was to illustrate how a person's thinking can pre-determine what they will do in a particular situation in the future.

Let me point out that these same probation officers who said they would keep the money would not steal from a store or another person or break into a car or home to steal. Why then would they keep the money from the teller? It is their thinking. One was associated with breaking the law while keeping the money was somebody's mistake, my gain.

In this situation, a person's behavior has been settled by how they think based on their values and beliefs. The situation presents an opportunity to test their character. The value that a person places on honesty will determine whether a person will return or keep the money. This scenario actually happened to me at my bank.

The youth and probation officers who said they would keep the money said it was the teller's mistake for giving them the extra money. To them it was not breaking the law, so they did not see keeping the money as stealing. Although they know it is not their money, they did not see keeping the money as being wrong. They were able to rationalize keeping the money as someone's mistake. In addition, both the adolescents and adults had a limited perspective as to the potential consequences for the teller. They did not see any.

The people who said they would give the money back cited two reasons for doing so. First, it was the bank's money, not theirs. Second, they recognized the teller would suffer harm by either having to pay the money back out of their pocket or lose their job.

Thinking determined how both groups of adolescents and adults would respond. Choices were made based on a set of values and beliefs that led to their decision when this unusual situation presented itself, the opportunity revealed the flaw in that person's thinking which led to their behavior.

A character flaw is different from a criminal who is continually thinking about taking what is not theirs from others. Whether it is a character flaw or a person's character, our thinking is behind how we got there.

Flawed thinking can be seen in people who are seemingly good people. It can be seen in lawyers who lie in court and misrepresent facts to get their clients out of trouble, judges and politicians who take a bribe behind the back, and husbands and wives who cheat on their spouses. They may otherwise be good people, but their flaw becomes a black eye on their overall character. If they are not careful, that flaw can spread like a disease and break down other aspects of their character.

Whether it is a character issue or a character flaw, some people are only willing to make changes when consequences come crashing down. Anything in your life that you are no longer in control of becomes Dr. Jekyll's serum. It can be things like excessive shopping and racking up a high amount of credit card debt, gambling, overeating, or hoarding. When you are no longer in control of your behavior, something has changed within you. When this happens, it is time to admit you need help whether it is to talk to a family member, a friend, or a therapist.

Understanding how your thinking has led you to where you are today, coupled with a strategy for changing your thinking, will go a long way in turning your life around.

# A Biblical Perspective on a Man's Heart

*"For as a man thinks in his heart, so is he."*
(Proverbs 23:7)

I want to return to the book of Genesis and focus on the thinking behind the story of Eve's temptation by the serpent, followed by the result.

The story begins with a conversation between the serpent and Eve. The serpent begins with a question, "... *Has God indeed said, you shall not eat of every tree of the garden?*" (Genesis 3:1.) The serpent is trying to put doubt into Eve's thinking on what God has said about the tree. Eve responds that God did indeed say this. The serpent presses ahead telling Eve that she is holding a false belief that God will punish her if she eats the fruit. He impugns God's nature by saying the only reason He said not to eat the fruit was to keep you from becoming like Him. (Genesis 3:1-6.)

Eve is persuaded to eat the fruit, which she then gives to Adam. This results in three changes. The first change is in man's relationship with God, the second is the change in the relationship between Adam and Eve, and finally the change in man's nature.

Adam and Eve who were created perfect, become imperfect. Their sinless nature is replaced with a sinful nature, which they will pass onto their children, who will then pass it on to each new generation after them. The result of their disobedience is, *"... for all have sinned and fall short of the glory of God."* (Romans 3:23.)

Removing the dialogue from this story, let us look at what the serpent did. He planted a thought into Eve's thinking to eat the fruit. This is how temptation begins, with a thought. Eve takes the serpent's words, thinks about them, and then forms a response as to whether she will eat the fruit. For Eve to respond to the serpent, she must understand what the serpent has said. If Eve rejects the serpent's offer there would be no more to the story. Instead, she leaves the door open for further discussion, which the serpent is more than happy to do.

Temptation can be external, like the serpent tempting Eve, or internal, created by your own thoughts and desires. Just like Eve, you are tempted by thoughts about things you know you should not do. And like Eve you must choose what you will do, or not do.

The connection between thinking and behavior is clearly laid out in this story. Once you understand the thinking-behavior connection, you can then see the need to continually check your thinking before making decisions.

Your thinking leads to the choices you make, shapes your character, and determines how you will live. As a Christian, who you are, followed by a Biblical standard of living should be shaped by the Bible and what it has to say about an issue.

One problem in the church today is people who are living together and then want to get married in a church. They may profess to be Christian people but are having premarital sex, choosing to overlook what the Bible has to say about this issue. They justify their behavior by saying "God knows we love one another." In their thinking that because they love each other, this somehow nullifies what God has to say regarding sexual behavior. The Bible is the only standard that is to be used to determine how Christians are to live in a relationship with God and one another.

Jesus addresses a different issue in how God's word can be stifled or nullified by church rules and regulations that are clearly outside of the Bible. You can see this is in various church or denominational rules and regulations that are not found in the Bible. Religious organizing is one of the biggest hindrances to the Holy Spirit freely working in our churches today. The story is found in Matthew 15:10-20.

Jesus is being questioned by the Pharisees as to why His disciples do not wash their hands before eating. The washing of hands is found in the tradition of the elders. These traditions were a subset of laws and rules that were outside of the Law of Moses, God's written word. They were considered to be extra-biblical. To the Pharisees, breaking these traditions was equal to breaking God's commandments. Therefore, the Pharisees considered the disciples to be unclean and unworthy of God's blessing in their life. Only if you keep their extra-biblical laws could you be considered righteous.

Jesus rebuffs the Pharisees by pointing out that eating with dirty hands does not defile a man, make him unclean. What goes into and comes out of a person's mouth are different issues. He explains that what goes into a person's mouth passes through the body and is expelled. This does not make a person unclean. Jesus clarifies that what makes a person unclean is what comes out of their mouth. What comes out of your mouth reveals something about you, because what comes out of your mouth comes from your heart.

## The Heart of Man

Jesus takes the Pharisees' concern for unwashed hands and redirects it to the real issue, the condition of a person's heart. The condition of man's heart needs to be the ultimate concern for a Christian believer.

Jesus, speaking to his followers, stated, "For out of the heart proceed evil thoughts, murders, adulteries, fornications, thefts, false witness, blasphemies." (Matthew 15:19.) Notice that evil thoughts precede a list of various behaviors, all of which break God's written law. Jesus points out that evil thoughts manifest in behavior. The behavior reveals the condition of a person's heart. A person's heart determines their character. Jesus is pointing out that every Christian should be concerned about the condition of their heart because the heart determines who you are and how you live.

King Solomon looks at the importance of the heart in the Proverbs, "As in water a face reflects face, so a man's heart reveals the man." (Proverbs 27:19.) Your heart reveals who you are and brings out things about you. When you can honestly take an inward look at yourself as if you were looking into a mirror, you will become aware of the changes you need to make in your life and in doing so, improve your relationship with God.

"Keep your heart with all diligence, for out of it spring the issues of life." (Proverbs 4:23.) The word keep could also be translated as *guard*, a military term that means "to stand watch over." This proverb commands the believer to stand watch over their heart. Why? Because the important decisions in life are made in relation to your heart condition. Therefore, you are to protect your heart by not letting things get in that will draw you away from God. When your heart is right, the choices you make will be right also. When your heart is not right, you can easily choose to ignore God's word, do what you want, and make a lot of mistakes.

## Flesh or Spirit: The True Dr. Jekyll, Mr. Hyde

Dr. Jekyll and Mr. Hyde could not coexist at the same time. Only one personality could be present at a time. This resulted in a battle for supremacy, who is going to rule and reign. This same type of battle rages within you and me. It is the battle between the flesh, which represents Mr. Hyde, and the spirit.

Paul speaks of a time when "… we all once conducted ourselves in the lusts of our flesh, fulfilling the desires of the flesh and of the mind, and were by nature children of wrath, just as the others." (Ephesians 2:3.) In this verse, Paul connects the behavior of the flesh to the desires of the mind. This is similar to Jesus placing evil thoughts in front of the bad behavior that follows.

Evil desires are the product of man's thinking and his imagination. Fantasy thinking fuels the desires of the flesh, which can lead to strong urges to act on them. Fantasy thinking is seen in various types of addictions, criminal behavior, as well as in sexual and violent behavior. If a person engages in fantasy thinking repeatedly, they are not far from acting on it.

Paul discusses the struggle between the flesh and the spirit in Romans chapter seven. He says that although he wants to do the right thing, he finds there is a struggle in him between doing the right thing versus the wrong thing. He describes this struggle as an ongoing battle as doing what is right and giving in to my fallen nature. It is a struggle that every Christian undergoes.

Paul provides an answer for how to overcome your fleshly desires. "For those who live according to the flesh set their minds on the things of the flesh, but those who live according to the Spirit, the things of the Spirit." (Romans 8:5.)

What you spend your time thinking about, (set your mind on,) determines how you live and whether you choose to focus on the flesh or the Spirit.

## Check Your Thinking

Jesus clearly states that bad behavior arises from evil thoughts that proceed out of the heart. As Christians, we need to take this seriously. I have seen, maybe you have too, Christians who have become trapped in some type of addiction, sexual sin, or bad behavior that has caused them to falter in their Christian walk.

These types of behaviors begin by entertaining specific thoughts or fantasies. These thoughts grow and eventually lead to a desire to act on them. Once you open the door to these thoughts, acting on them is not far behind.

The process of turning a thought into imagination and then into behavior can be seen in a person who has gotten caught up in adultery. Adultery begins with one thought. This thought grows as a person begins to flirt with the idea. Over time their thoughts extend to periods of time thinking about the person they want to be involved with and how to make it happen.

Little behaviors begin to manifest such as flirting and consciously putting yourself in the proximity of this person. You begin to hide things from your spouse. These behaviors can titillate and reinforce sexual desire. At this point, the person is not far from committing adultery. What did Proverbs say about going down this path? To guard your heart.

The pattern I have described regarding a person who is moving toward committing adultery is the same pattern for every type of temptation that pulls you away from staying true to God's word.

If you have already acted on your thoughts and fantasies in the past you will need to repent and confess what you have done. You need to ask God to forgive you. Only by doing this can you be set free from this behavior and the guilt you feel so that you do not repeat it in the future. Keeping it a secret only allows it to continue. There is an emotional toll on the person who keeps their sin a secret. You may also need to confess your sin to a Christian brother or sister who can pray with you and hold you accountable in the future.

## How We Think About Ourselves

Another area of concern is how we think about ourselves in relation to others. Paul tells us,

"... not to think of himself more highly than he ought to think, but to think soberly as God has dealt to each one a measure of faith." (Romans 12:3.) Soberly means having sound judgment.

Paul is warning all Christians not to have an inflated sense of self which he likens to drunkenness. Drunkenness leads to not being able to think clearly. Paul warns against thinking that causes you to see yourself unclearly and as being better than other people.

Thinking soberly and with good judgment means knowing who you are in Christ, and how you are to relate to others. A healthy view of self means that although you may have different talents and abilities than others, live at a different socio-economic level to others, or have a position of authority or prominence, you are not better than others, only with different responsibilities. This was the problem the Pharisees had because they were religious elites. They thought of themselves as better than the common people they ministered to. They had a religious superiority complex. In God's eyes, we are all equal; no one is better than another.

## Comparing Ourselves to Others

Thinking we are better than others can be seen when we compare ourselves to other people. When we do this, we put people at different levels, who is higher, who is lower, and where I fit in. This is all based on perception, which we learned earlier is not always accurate.

I am sure some of you may have felt looked down upon by someone at some point in your life. If you are honest about this, maybe you have done this to someone else. How do you look at the homeless and those that stand on street corners with signs asking for help? What do you say to yourself about them?

Paul is warning us not to think of ourselves as better than others. The guiding principle for each of us should be love. If God loves us all equally then He does not love me more than them. I am not better in God's eyes than them.

The Bible encourages us to love one another. When Jesus was asked what the greatest commandment is, He replied by connecting the first commandment of loving God, to the second commandment of loving your neighbor as yourself. We will have difficulty loving others if we see ourselves as being better than others and sit in judgment on them.

Paul expands on how we are to treat others.

- "Be of the same mind toward one another. Do not set your mind on high things but associate with the humble. Do not be wise in your own opinion." (Romans 12:16.)
- "Repay no one evil for evil. Have regard for good things in the sight of all men." (Romans 12:17.)

Jesus went even further in how we are to treat others. "But I say to you love your enemies, bless those who persecute you, do good to those who hate you, and pray for those who spitefully use you and persecute you." (Matthew 5:44.) How we treat people goes much deeper than just behavior. It strikes at the core of our heart and character, then our behavior.

## Thinking and Choices

"Finally brethren, whatever things are true, whatever things are noble, whatever things are just, whatever things are pure, whatever things are lovely, whatever things are of good report, if there is any virtue and if there is anything praiseworthy—meditate on these things." (Philippians 4:8.)

I want to take you back to what I said about thoughts. You get to choose what thoughts you think about and what you spend your time thinking on.

The word meditate means to deeply think upon, to ponder. Paul is telling the Philippians that they have a choice in what they choose to think about during the day. He points out several positive things that you can spend your time thinking about and meditating on.

The first Psalm points out that a Christian who meditates on God's word night and day will be blessed by God. This blessing includes stability, fruitfulness, times of refreshing, and prosperity. These blessings are closely connected to reading and meditating on God's word.

Very few Christians take time to read the word of God with any consistency. Only about one in ten Christians read their Bible every day. What about you? What are you filling your mind with? The reality that only ten percent of Christians read their Bible daily may explain why so few Christians make regular progress in their Christian walk, struggle with unbelief, and get stuck in various sins they have difficulty overcoming. Meditating in God's word strengthens you in times of temptation and helps to counteract the negative influences that are all around you.

If you are filling your mind with the same thinking that got you where you are today, then you will continue to stay stuck. There is a saying, garbage in, garbage out. Some of you may need to reevaluate the things that are consuming your time and filling your thoughts. Picking up your Bible is a good starting point for filling your mind with positive thoughts and learning more about God's love and plan for you.

# Thinking Strategies

*"A new way of thinking has become the necessary condition for responsible living and acting."*
-Dalai Lama

The importance of thinking cannot be overstressed. If you are not happy with where your life is at this moment in time, you have the power to change it.

To help you look at how to make changes in your thinking we began by looking at the different components involved in your thinking. Now we will look at some thinking strategies to change how you think. Many of the adolescents and adults I worked with had poor problem-solving skills. Learning new skills can help you develop new strategies for making changes in your life.

## Contemplation

Contemplation is focused thinking, meaning, to think on something thoughtfully for an extended period of time. There is a proverb of a man who goes for a walk in his neighborhood. As he does, he walks past his neighbor's house and sees that the neighbor's field is uncared for and that the wall that surrounds his property is in a state of disrepair.

The man stops to take a few minutes to think about what he sees. "When I saw it, I considered it well; I looked on it and received instruction:" (Proverbs 24:32.) The words considered it well could be replaced with the word contemplated. To take time to contemplate the man needed to slow down and stop what he was doing. What life lesson might he learn by looking at his neighbor's yard?

Contemplation requires you to look at what is going on around you. The purpose is to see if you can learn something from what you are seeing and apply it to your life. Looking at the neighbor's yard can become a life lesson to teach you something.

Contemplation can help you learn from your mistakes, as well as the mistakes of others.

"Ponder the path of your feet, and let your ways be established." (Proverbs 4:26.) Ponder means to watch, consider, examine, and think upon. Ponder means to take the time to think through to a conclusion. As you spend time thinking about the choices in front of you, the path of your feet, you are to spend time weighing the decision you will make. You will always stand on solid ground if you take the time to contemplate what you are going to do before you do it.

Contemplation is meant to teach you and give you an understanding about getting all the right information you need. Then apply it to how are you going to make it happen. Life is filled with object lessons that if you take the time to look for them, will teach you a better way of living.

## Self-Reflective Thinking

A reflection is an image of an object, it is not the object. When you stand in front of a mirror it reflects back what you look like. If your hair is a mess, or you have a pimple on your face, you become aware of it.

Self-reflective thinking means taking an inward look at yourself. Self-reflection is meant to reveal what is inside of you. Self-reflection can help you to see the positive things you are doing and need to keep doing, and the negative things you need to stop doing.

Self-reflection can help you take a historical look at your life and see the things that have made you who you are and how you got to where you are today. Self-reflection can also help you look ahead at where you want to be tomorrow. Like contemplation, self-reflection is meant to teach and instruct you.

Contemplation and self-reflection take time to do. You cannot rush through them if you want to benefit from them. Most people are not used to taking the time to think, contemplate, self-reflect, and explore their thinking. But the rewards of having the time to do so are big.

## Corrective Thinking

The formula for correcting thinking as you have learned is *"thinking leads to choices, choices lead to behavior, behavior leads to consequences."* It is a simple formula that I recommend you commit to memory.

The best way to use this thinking approach is to work backward. You start with the end result of your behavior, the consequences. Starting with the consequences will reinforce your need to change. Think for a moment of bad behavior that has led to some negative consequences recently. Take the time to write them down. Negative consequences are the cost of your bad behavior, the price you pay when you do something wrong or stupid.

To make this point in my corrective thinking classes, I used the concept of having money to buy new clothes. An adolescent is given fifty dollars to buy clothes. One store has a pair of brand-name jeans they really want, but the pants will take all their money to buy them. At the next store, there are two really cool shirts and a pair of jeans that are nice, but not as cool as the ones at the other store. The two T-shirts and pair of pants cost fifty dollars. Which store will you buy from? The lesson is meant to teach the necessity of weighing the cost of behavior before they act.

If you will take the time to weigh the consequences of your choices before you act you will start making better choices. Better choices will lead to less pain in life. I would ask probation kids if they thought that the consequences they were suffering; being arrested, incarcerated, and put on probation was worth the price they were paying for what they did? Some of them, believe it or not, said yes.

From consequences, you move to the behavior that caused those consequences. The focus is on your behavior, not what other people did. You need to be honest about what you did or said. Do not lie to yourself or try to excuse what you did by blaming someone or something else. Identifying the bad behavior that led to the consequence should be fairly easy to do.

From behavior, you move to choices. Take a minute to see if there were different choices you could have made at the time you acted but did not. Write them down. Add to this list the choices that you can see now that you could have made. Sometimes after we get out of a situation, we realize there were other choices that could have been made. The object is to come up with as many choices that were available if you had taken the time to think. This exercise teaches you how to look for solutions the next time you get into a similar circumstance. As you look at the other choices you could have made, hopefully, this will teach you that there are many choices available in the future, not just one.

This takes us to the true starting point of what happened, the thinking that led to your choice and behavior. Working backward helps you clearly see the consequences of your choices and behavior. Once you have done this, you can now focus on the thinking that led to your choosing bad behavior. Your thinking is what created the problem in the first place.

An incident that happened recently illustrates how quickly emotions can escalate when people are reacting and not thinking. In this example, I will use italics to identify the thinking behind what is going on in this incident.

Bill was at a movie theater when his young son needed to use the restroom. The restroom contains numerous adult urinals, but only one child's urinal. There were also stalls with toilets available. When Bill walked into the restroom there was only one adult in there at the time, and he was using the child's urinal. My friend's son urgently needed to go to the bathroom. All Bill could see at this point was an adult using the child's urinal. *The stimulus is the adult using this urinal.* Bill becomes angry quickly over this. *The stimulus leads to an emotional reaction.*

Bill's anger leads to him confronting the man. *Bill's anger has created tunnel vision. He is not looking for other choices available to him.* The confrontation quickly escalates toward a fight. *Bill's anger leads to an immediate emotional behavior by confronting the other man. He chooses not to let this issue go, walk away, and look for another option.*

The other person pauses, looks at Bill and then his son, and says, "If your son was not here, I would give you a beat down." The fight has been diverted, but no thanks to Bill. Bill returns to his seat angrily and decides to share his story with me. *He is now choosing to retell his story, which will keep his anger going.*

When asked, most people would answer that the man using the only child's urinal made Bill angry. Beep, wrong answer! What made Bill angry was his thinking about the man using the child urinal.

Bill had a belief that he openly shared with me when I asked why he felt he needed to say anything to the man. To Bill, this man was clearly ignorant and he felt he needed to do something to correct him. *Bill is no longer thinking rationally.*

Bill had other choices he could have made. He could have taken his son to a toilet stall, which was empty at the time. He could have waited until the man was done. *Tunnel Vision blocked him from seeing other options.* Being angry limited his ability to think beyond what was happening. Bill was focused on the person who caused him to become angry.

Bill lost sight of the potential outcome of choosing to get into a confrontation with the other person. *Bill is not thinking through his choices to the potential consequences.* If he gets into a fight with this man, he could be arrested. What about the effect the fight would have had on his son? That was nowhere in his thinking. Once Bill's anger kicked in, he only saw one solution.

To be able to learn from your experiences means you have to understand your thinking behind what is going on. By simply saying the man using the child's urinal created his anger teaches Bill nothing about himself. He will not learn how to avoid a similar situation in the future. If Bill does not learn from these types of interactions, he will continue to make the same types of mistakes in the future. Next time the consequences may not be avoided.

## Problem-Solving

Problem-solving is exactly what it sounds like. It is meant to help you develop a strategy to solve a problem or change a behavior. There are four basic steps in problem-solving:

1. Identify and define the problem. To find solutions to your problems you must first have a clear understanding of what the real problem is.
2. Gather information and brainstorm ideas. Gathering information is an easy thing to do based on the amount of information available on the internet. When I personally need to look up information regarding different topics, I get on the Internet to look for answers. How many of you have used a YouTube video to learn how to fix something that was broken? There is information available for almost any topic or problem you will encounter in life.

Brainstorming is coming up with a list of as many ideas as you can think of, things that could possibly help solve the problem. What you do here is simply make a list of options. Do not rule anything out or try to determine if it is a good or bad idea.

3. Explore different solutions and select one. First, go over your list of options and eliminate any ideas that are impractical as well as options that cannot be implemented right now. For instance, if one of the ideas you came up with would cost you the money you do not have right now, then it is not a practical solution at this time. However, you should set this idea aside for review at a later time when you are in a better position financially to use it. Eliminate as many ideas as you can to thin your list down.

   Next take the things that are left on the list, prioritize by identifying the options that you can implement right away. Sometimes it may be only one thing, other times you may be able to find multiple things you can do. Prioritize your list beginning with your first and best choice. There may be multiple things you can do at the same time, but you still need to pick your first and best choice to get started. The one that you know you can do right now.

4. Take action and stick with it. The time for excuses is over. It is time to act and put your plan into action. You may find that when you start to work on the problem it might be tougher than you thought. This is normal. Overcoming a period in your life where you have become comfortable can prove to be a struggle. Self-control is not easy when you have not practiced it for a while.

Problem-solving is a step-by-step process that helps you look at problems, identify solutions, and implement action steps.

## Critical Thinking

In using the term critical thinking, I am not using it in a scholarly way. I am using a simple definition, which is at the core of critical thinking. Critical thinking is objective thinking; the ability to analyze information to form an opinion or make a judgment based on facts. Critical thinking is free from emotions.

Critical thinking is not based on what you feel. Emotions impair your ability to evaluate yourself and what is going on around you. You will find that there is a difference in how you think when you are calm and have had the time to think about what happened, versus how you think when you are emotionally reactive. Your thinking will definitely be clearer after you have had time to set your emotions aside. This is necessary for critical thinking.

Critical thinking can only be helpful when it is based on facts, accurate and realistic. Critical thinking is not based on guesses. You need to have information that backs it up.

Critical thinking must be an honest exploration of your thinking, beginning with taking the responsibility for what you said or did. There can be no excuses or blaming others for what has happened. The focus is on yourself; how you behaved, reacted, and thought. If you cannot be honest with yourself, critical thinking does not work.

Finally, critical thinking is not subjective. In an old-time TV police show, the detective would always say to the person he was interviewing, "Just the facts ma'am." The objective fact is free of a person's opinion.

I want to use a brief example to look at how critical thinking works with a false belief. If you look at the world and believe everyone should be nice, and somebody mistreats you, critical thinking looks at the false belief to help change it. Why? Because in the real world not everyone is nice.

Learning to be objective is foundational in critical thinking and is meant to help you look at yourself honestly.

This chapter is meant to give you some strategies in order to help you change your thinking, control your emotions and behavior, and live a prosperous life.

# Difficult Emotions

*"Learning to control an immediate emotional reaction is the starting point in learning to control an emotion you struggle with repeatedly."*
-Brad Garrett

## Overcoming Difficult Emotions

When you repeatedly have a reaction with an emotion like anger, stress, or anxiousness, a pattern develops and increases the likelihood you will respond this way in the future. Over time, the response becomes programmed making it difficult for you to control the emotion, even though you may be able to maintain control over your other emotions.

To clarify what may be obvious, there is a difference between an emotional reaction like anger and a person who repeatedly struggles with anger. This is true for all of the negative emotions. Most people have typical emotional reactions that they are able to control most of the time. The person who repeatedly struggles with one emotion has become programmed in their response.

People whose emotional response has become programmed over time will function on a daily basis at a higher level of anger, stress, or anxiousness than the average person. There were some kids I saw on probation whose anger always seemed to simmer just below the surface. It was as if their anger was waiting for opportunities to come out. These teenagers responded more often with anger than their peers did, were more aggressive, and more violent than others when they became angry.

A person who repeatedly struggles with one particular emotion is more emotionally sensitive and reactive than others are to the same emotion. Increased sensitivity leads to getting angry quicker, stressed faster, or anxious more often than most people do. A person who has good emotional control does not give a second thought to many of the things that happen to them throughout the day compared to people who have become more emotionally sensitive.

Emotionally sensitive people react to small things, where for others it may not even register as an issue. When asked, these people typically rate their emotional scale scores at a higher level than others. There were some kids I worked with who always reacted at a level nine or ten with anger, stress, or anxiousness. There are some adults I know who regularly have elevated levels of stress when compared to others.

Angry people tend to stay angry longer, while people who struggle with stress go from one crisis to the next. A person who struggles with a specific emotion will have more difficulty learning how to control that emotion. As you move forward focus on one high-energy negative emotion you struggle with and want to learn to control.

Controlling a difficult emotion begins by repeatedly stopping that emotion each time you feel the urge to react.

## Rational Emotive Behavior Therapy (REBT)

REBT began in the 1950s as rational therapy, which was developed by Albert Ellis, PhD. Rational therapy later became Rational Emotive Therapy with an emphasis on helping people learn to control their emotions. Later the B was added to cover behavior. Dr. Ellis was the first psychologist to create a therapy that focused on controlling emotions and the behavior that followed by addressing a person's thinking.

Dr. Ellis stated regarding people's emotional reactions, "People don't just get upset. They contribute to their upsetness."

REBT provides people with a way to look at the thinking behind the emotion.

By reading this book, you have become aware of some of the things you can do to help control your emotional reactions in the future. If you continue to react in a similar way you have in the past, then you are doing what Dr. Ellis alluded to, you are contributing to your emotional distress.

A quick example of choosing not to control an emotion is when a person believes it is more important to argue with someone to prove a point than it is to calm down. Some people feel it is more important to prove they are right than it is to control what they are feeling. This only reinforces that your pattern of emotionally responding will continue.

## How Emotions Are Formed

Your brain is a storehouse of past experiences, memories, education, and thinking. The amygdala is the storehouse for emotional memories. Emotional memories play a role in emotional reactions in the present time. This can be illustrated by using music. Think of a song related to a past relationship you had. Does a particular feeling come with that song reminding you of a particular experience? If it does, that memory was in the amygdala storehouse.

The type of emotional memory you have depends on whether it was a good or bad experience. It is important to understand how an emotional memory can have an effect on you in the present.

These past memories become a basis for how your amygdala interprets a stimulus and responds in the present. It is like déjà vu with emotions, been here, done that, know how to react. How you react emotionally to a person or a current situation in the present can be based on your past experiences and memories. You are not even aware of when this is happening most of the time.

These memories work at a non-conscious level. They are able to influence how the amygdala interprets a stimulus. Past emotional experiences form the basis for how you will react in the present.

## Theme-Thinking

The problem behind difficult emotions you repeatedly struggle with is the programmed response. There will always be some room for variation in how and when you respond. What started out a long time ago as a normal emotional reaction, through a repeated pattern of how you responded, programmed your brain in how to react. In a similar way to fight-or-flight where the zebra runs most of the time, you have created a response pattern that will be followed most of the time.

One way to look at a repetitious emotional reaction is through theme thinking. Theme thinking looks at the people, places, and circumstances in which your reactions regularly occur. The question is what do people, places, or circumstances have in common? For instance, there can be a certain personality type that always seems to get to you, certain types of places where you become anxious, or a certain type of issue that repeatedly causes you stress. What these things have in the common form a theme. I want to use a hypothetical situation to illustrate how this works.

Joe enters counseling to deal with an anger problem. He has not had a problem in the past with anger. He identifies his anger started while he is going through a very difficult divorce that began when he found out his wife was cheating on him. His anger response could be considered a normal reaction for people who have had a similar experience.

Over the course of the next couple of years, Joe begins and ends two different relationships. Joe had difficulty with his anger in both relationships. The breakups reinforce his anger and result in reinforcing a perception and belief he has regarding women. This began with his divorce.

During this period of time, he is fired from his job by a female boss. Although he was highly qualified for this position, certain issues keep coming up regarding his interactions with female employees, including his boss.

Teaching Joe anger management skills may help him control his anger, but it does not get at his real problem. The first question needing to be asked is when did Joe's anger first appear?

Next, is his anger generalized, or does it appear with specific people or certain genders? In what circumstances does his anger arise?

After a brief exploration it is found that his anger began with the divorce, only arises with females, and can appear in any type of situation where a woman is involved. Joe has developed a belief in how he sees and relates to women. Based on this information we have found common elements related to his anger that form a theme.

To resolve his anger issue, he will need to address his anger toward his ex-wife. Forgiveness is a good idea. If he can do this, he will be able to look at his relationships and belief/s about women. Then he can more honestly look at how he contributed to the relationship failure. Simply teaching him some anger management skills is not going to solve his problem.

Although what is happening in the present is not the same as something that has happened in the past, it may have similarities to it. Similarities and commonalities to past experiences form the theme in the present.

I see this often with probation kids who have serious problems with authority. This problem started by rebelling against their parent's authority. From there it spreads like a disease to teachers, principals, law enforcement, and eventually bosses at work. It does not matter who the person is, only that they are in a position of power.

Behind this attitude are the emotions and thinking that support their attitude and behavior. They react to all authority without knowing anything about what the person is like who has the authority. These adolescents believe there is nothing wrong with the way they think or behave toward these people. What started out as an emotional reaction to their parent's authority grew to where it applies to all authority. However, even some of these kids may have an exception to this behavior, such as one teacher they like.

The adolescent's reaction in this example is no longer just a part of an emotional reaction. It has now grown into a problematic emotion with an attitude and behavior attached to it that becomes their normal way of responding. Any emotion you repeatedly struggle with becomes your normal way of responding. Theme thinking is meant to help you look for all the similarities and commonalities that people, places, and circumstances have in common with the emotion you struggle with.

## How You Think About an Emotion

What you believe about emotions, in general, or about a specific emotion you struggle with will have an effect on your approach to controlling your emotions. If you believe that anger is good because it helps you get what you want, you are probably not going to give up your anger any time soon. If something helps you get what you want, there is little motivation to give it up.

If you believe stress is normal, or that it goes away on its own when the problem is over, you probably will not see a need to control your stress. It will be difficult for you to see the benefits that could come with less stress in your life. I have heard it said that some stress can be good. If you believe this, okay. What I have found is that I can still resolve problems without having to feel stressed out to do it. Stress does not help you solve problems, if anything, it creates a different set of problems for you.

If you have a belief that depression and anxiety can only be controlled through medication, you will not be motivated to learn about depression or anxiety and do things for yourself that can help you overcome these issues without medication.

Education about specific emotions can help you understand how they work and what you can do for yourself. The more you understand about emotions, combined with the knowledge you gain about yourself through self-examination, the more capable you become in controlling that stubborn emotion.

Overcoming a difficult emotion requires you to put in some work. It is similar to going to the gym to exercise for good health. Lifting weights builds muscles. Practicing new things you have learned, coupled with practicing self-control will help you build emotional muscle control.

## Traffic: To React or Not React

There are a wide variety of negative emotions you might feel while driving in your car on any given day. These emotions can range from frustration and irritation to outright anger or stress. Driving in traffic can be stressful. There are time demands that require you to get from one place to the next on time. Then there are the other drivers you must deal with.

To make the change in how I drive, I took a theme approach. I wanted to know what was causing me to react negatively so often. I knew that it was not what was going on outside of my car that was causing me to react, it was what was going on inside of me that was causing the reaction.

As I thought about driving, I discovered there was one theme that played into my emotional reactions. Listed below are the changes

I had to make in my thinking first, which then translated into a change in my behavior.

- My reactions were occurring with all drivers and in any situation. The theme formed a belief that I was the only one that knew how people should drive. The first change I had to make was in my thinking. Everybody has the right to drive however they want to no matter what I think.
- Second: I had to consciously take my eyes off the negative things and people that come with driving a car.
- Third: I had to learn the difference between the things I could and could not control while driving. I had to let go of the people and situations that come up while driving that I cannot control. I shifted my focus to the things I could control, which were inside my car, not outside.
- I practiced yoga breathing while driving to help me keep my emotions in check. I wanted to remain calm so I could enjoy the ride. I knew that breathing would help me do this. I put more focus on the music in my car and the scenery outside my car.

I want to be clear that I still have the ability to react emotionally while driving. But by making a conscious choice each time I get in my car to drive, and then repeatedly practicing the things I know to do, the negative emotional reactions will be kept in check. The change began when I challenged my thinking about what driving a car should feel like.

People tend to hold on to certain things in their life and the negative emotions that come with them. Most of these things could be changed at any time by simply challenging how you think and the effect it is having on your life. If you had a pebble in your shoe, would you keep walking on it? And yet you may live with the negative consequences that come with not taking control of situations and controlling your emotions.

## Traffic: One Repeating Event, One Emotion

One person I was counseling with had recently become aware of how much stress he was creating for himself in getting to work each morning. The problem was that he would wait until the last minute before leaving the house for work. It had become a habit.

The emotional stress he felt was created by putting himself into a very tight situation. The problem behavior is easy to identify and the consequence for doing this was a repetitive emotional stress reaction. The stress could also intensify if the traffic was bad that morning.

His thinking was clearly unrealistic and somewhat magical. He believed he could wait until the last minute and that everything would go smoothly. If he approaches driving this way on other occasions, then this problem has generalized to every situation where he needs to get somewhere on time. However, it was only limited to getting to work.

As he became aware of the stress he was creating for himself, he set a goal of driving to work stress-free. To make this happen, one thought needed to change; it is not okay to wait until the last minute to go to work. He made a decision to leave home a few minutes earlier each day to avoid the stress he was creating for himself. He reset his mental clock and changed his behavior. Once this was done, the stress was gone, the drive became more pleasant, and he arrived at work stress-free. If he continues to do this for about thirty days, this will become the way he drives to work from now on. An interesting note here is that learning to control one stressor opens the door to making other changes that are caused by stress.

Changing just one thought, followed by changing the behavior that went with it, improved his life. It does not matter why they thought it was okay to wait until the last minute. What did matter was to connect the thought that it was okay to wait until the last minute, with the stress that came with it? This gave him the understanding that making one simple choice could improve his life. Making one small improvement in your life can open the door to resolving other issues that may cause you to feel stress, anger, and anxiousness.

## Grief

Two youth experience the same circumstance, their father's death. The two boy's fathers die when they are fifteen years old. The first boy has had a very close relationship with his biological father whom he has lived with, along with his mother and two younger siblings, until his father's death. His family is close and is supportive of one another.

The second boy's father left home when he was five years old. He has not heard from his father since that time. He has just been made aware his biological father died recently. This boy lives at home with his mother and two siblings, each of whom has a different father. His family is not close. Unfortunately, the second boy's story was not unusual where I work.

How will these two boys react to the news of their father's death? How they react depends on how they think about their father, which is based on the type of relationship they had with him.

The first boy who has had a close relationship with his father will feel grief. Why? Because his relationship with his father was close and supportive. His grief includes knowing he will not be able to have a relationship with his father as he grows older, and that his father will not be able to see him graduate, go to college, or get married. His children will never be able to meet their grandfather. All these thoughts play into his feelings of grief.

The second boy did not have a relationship with his father. He will not experience the same feelings as the first boy about his father. He may or may not experience grief. In fact, any feelings of grief he may have might have been attached to what he felt when his father left home. Many of the kids I worked with have negative feelings about their father due to how this scenario played out in their lives.

Many of them said they had quit thinking about their father a long time ago. They no longer had a need for him to be in their life since he was not there when they needed him. This boy had learned how to live without his father. How each boy thinks about their father determines their level of grief.

I think many people look at grief as something that gradually goes away on its own. This could not be farther from the truth. It is true that time does distance us from emotional pain, but it does not resolve it. What can be missed in the grief process is how a person's thinking about the person's death changes over time. As they grieve, they are working through the loss. Over time the person gives themself permission to stop grieving.

A person chooses, whether conscious or unconscious, how long they will grieve. How long is the right amount of time to grieve? How long should a person wait after the death of their spouse before they date or marry? If emotion can change over time without consciously thinking about it, how much quicker can an emotion change that you are consciously thinking about and working on. The situation does not have to change, to change how you feel about the situation.

## Distress

Distress is defined as unhappiness, pain, or suffering that affects the mind and body. This last example is a little trickier to understand the thinking because distress, and the behavior that came with it, was the result of what he believed about himself.

I once worked with a young man who believed he smelled bad. That was not the reason I was seeing him, but it came up as a problem we worked on together. Believing he smelled bad resulted in feeling distressed more days than not. Because of this, he became extremely self-conscious. This led to minimizing his interaction with peers, which created some feelings of loneliness and sadness.

Joe did all the right things he needed to do for good hygiene. He took showers, brushed his teeth, used deodorant, and would wear clean clothes to ensure he would not smell bad. But in spite of this, he continued to believe he smelled bad. This belief caused him to continually smell his clothing and to blow into his hand to check his breath.

When he walked past kids at school, he thought they were talking about him if they looked his way. The same was true if he walked up to people who were talking and then would quiet down when he joined them. They must have been talking about me he thought. And if there happened to be a strange smell when he was around people, he believed that it must be him. This problem began small but developed into an ongoing issue.

One of the first things I did each counseling session was to intentionally smell him, of course asking permission. I would then say you smell fine. If the parent was in the session, I would have them smell too. They would say the same thing, you smell fine. I had him smell himself and then tell me if there was a problem. He still believed he smelled bad even after the parent and I told him he did not. The purpose of this intervention was to provide contradictory information to him, and his belief about himself.

Next, I would ask if he thought his parent or myself were lying about not smelling bad. This was to challenge the internal belief about himself. The contradictory information was coming from two different people he trusted. He had to decide whether we were telling the truth or lying. He believed we were telling the truth, but even with that, it took some time for him to believe he did not smell bad.

We talked about misreading social cues. We looked at how he came up with the thought he knows what people are thinking. He finally had to admit that there was no way he could know what other people were thinking without asking them. The only thing he could do was guess at what they were doing or thinking, which could be incorrect.

Joe's thought—he smelled bad; true or false, rational or irrational—created how he felt about himself. Joe did not need people to cause him to feel distressed and unhappy. He did that to himself. The people were props that allowed him to continue in his belief he smelled bad.

Although this is an unusual story, how many of you have experienced a negative emotion based on what you believe about yourself? How many of you believe you are not good enough, smart enough, attractive enough, or think that you are a loser? It does not take people to cause you to feel this way, you can make yourself feel this way.

The key to dealing with this type of emotional problem is to recognize the beliefs and thinking behind the negative feelings you have about yourself. Once you do this you need to address them. You may need to have some family or friends around who can be objective and offer support. Positive affirmations from others are important. Anyone who has lost weight knows how good a positive affirmation feels.

You will need to quit looking for the negative things in your life that support your false beliefs about yourself. Then stop the negative self-talk that contributes to how you feel about yourself. You need to look for all the positive things in yourself that will contradict every negative view and belief you have about yourself. You are valuable as a person. Your self-worth comes from God and the life He has given you.

# Problem Behavior

*"Learn from the mistakes of others. You can never live long enough to make them all yourself."*
-Groucho Marx

In a similar way that we separated an emotional reaction from one specific problematic emotion, we are now going to separate problem behavior from the behavior that comes with an emotional reaction. Some of the things we will look at in this chapter will be familiar, other aspects will be new.

The process for changing bad behavior begins with awareness of the thinking behind the behavior. My Thinking > creates > My Problem Behavior.

Gambling can be a serious problem behavior for some people, especially for those who live in Las Vegas, Nevada. Gambling behavior, when it first begins, is not the result of an emotional reaction. Most people start gambling innocently enough by putting twenty dollars in a video poker machine, playing Blackjack or Craps, or betting on football. Gambling begins as a curiosity or a choice for fun.

Although gambling does not begin as emotional behavior, problem gambling can lead to a host of troubling emotions. One of the most serious consequences of problem gambling can be seen in the people who have committed suicide after sustaining large financial losses. A lesser consequence of gambling is the stress that is created by gambling losses. I personally know people who have lost their paycheck gambling and then had to go through the emotional turmoil that was created when they did not have the money to pay their bills.

> *A negative emotional response can lead to bad behavior,*
> *and bad behavior by itself can lead to*
> *a negative emotional response.*

Bad behavior creates its own set of negative emotions. The person who loses their paycheck gambling will feel emotions such as stress over the loss, depression, or anger at themselves for having done this. The stress will be magnified later when there is no money to pay the bills, get gas for the car, or buy groceries. The stress did not create the behavior, the behavior created the stress.

There is a term used in gambling that reveals a person may be developing a gambling problem. It is called chasing your money, meaning your losses. When this happens, the stress they feel from the losses encourages them to gamble again with the hope they will recover those losses.

Through this type of repeated experience, an emotion like stress can become attached to the gambling behavior. When this happens, the person may associate feelings of stress with thoughts of gambling. When emotion becomes attached to behavior, a neural pathway is created in the brain, making it easier to gamble in the future the next time they feel stressed.

People who have developed a gambling problem feel strong urges to gamble. People may gamble to escape stress but feel more stress if they lose. This is no different from drug or alcohol use or sexual behavior. Gambling can create an urge that encourages the behavior even when a person is not near a casino. With addictions, it is the thought first, creating an urge similar to an emotion, then the behavior follows.

## Behavior: An Overview

We know that bad behavior can come with an emotional reaction. But you never need to feel an emotion to behave badly. For instance, there are people who have no difficulty lying to others, even repeatedly. Some people steal, drink and drive, abuse drugs, cheat on their spouses, and cuss like sailors. They do not need to feel an emotion to engage in bad behavior, only a thought. A lot of people who do these things do not see these behaviors as a problem for them.

For most people, bad behavior only changes when negative consequences are attached to them. If you lie to a family member or a friend, if you steal something from another person, or cheat on your spouse, without feeling some type of negative emotional reaction or having consequences attached to your behavior there is not much to encourage change.

One young man who was in my anger management group admitted his family does not want him around their family bar-b-ques because of his anger. Hopefully, the rejection by his family keeping him from attending family functions will be enough to change his anger and angry behavior. But if not, who knows what consequences will need to take place to change his mind about his anger.

There are problem behaviors like drug or alcohol use that can easily turn into an addiction. The addiction begins to create emotional problems as the drug and alcohol use continues. Prior to full-blown addiction, negative consequences can be seen as the person begins abusing the drug. Drug use can lead to negative emotions like stress, anxiety, or depression over time. Drug abuse may wreak havoc in their relationships, but for some people, this may not be enough to want to change.

Another type of bad behavior that can create negative emotions is procrastination. The negative emotions are caused by repeatedly putting off doing things that are needed to be done now. If a time deadline is involved, say a school or work project, the procrastination creates unnecessary stress that could have been avoided by working on the project earlier. The more a person puts off something they need to do; the intensity of the negative emotion will increase until they finally address what needs to be done.

Similar to procrastination is disorganization. Disorganization can be seen as a pattern of behavior in people who either take on projects without any forethought or planning, as well as those who live in unnecessary clutter. Disorganization can lead to a person's plans failing to materialize. In this type of disorganization, a person simply fails to plan ahead and be aware of potential problems that could develop as they go forward. The consequences that can result from this failure are that projects can cost more and take longer to complete. Sometimes, disorganization can mean those projects never get completed.

Disorganization can also lead to not being able to find things like tools when you need them. When this happens, it leads to an emotional reaction, and possibly blaming everybody and their children, but never yourself when you fail to find what you are looking for.

Disorganization can lead to frustration or anger when there is something important you need to find and cannot find it. Have you ever watched someone who misplaced something look for it? Every so often this happens with one of my sons. When he cannot find what he is looking for he becomes frustrated and starts cussing, as if cussing is going to help him find it.

A similar type of scenario can be seen in a person who is financially disorganized and does not know how to manage their money. If they do not learn how to manage their money, they will continue to experience ongoing money problems, as well as the stress that goes with it.

## Emotions and Bad Behavior

People who struggle with stress, anger, or anxiety have choices in how they will deal with these emotions. Drug and alcohol use was a common way that adolescents on probation used to deal with their emotions. These kids would self-medicate as a way to deal with the emotional problems they were experiencing. Adults also self-medicate by using alcohol or drugs to deal with their emotions. In drug behavior, we call this "numbing yourself."

A lot of people have a tough time dealing with reality and the problems that come with life. When a person starts to use substances to deal with life, a new set of problems develop. The new problems bring a new set of negative emotional responses that go with them. To stop this from happening it is necessary to find healthy and positive ways to fill the vacuum when you stop the behavior.

Viewing pornography can become a serious problem behavior just like gambling. Both can develop into an addiction over time. Both of these behaviors can lead to marital and relationship problems, even ending in a breakup or divorce. They also bring with them a host of negative emotions and problems that will affect your life and your family.

A problem behavior I saw with probation youth, mostly girls, was self-mutilation. These young girls would use knives or razors to cut on their arms and legs. Many of these kids used self-mutilation to escape from the stress, anger, and anxiety they were experiencing in their lives.

Although their emotions lead them to self-mutilate as a way to deal with what they were going through, it also created a whole different set of problems and negative emotions for them, shame for one, as they dressed to hide the damage they had done to their bodies. Unfortunately, self-mutilation can actually work in relieving the negative emotions they felt, but only temporarily.

You have learned that an emotional reaction comes with emotional behavior. Now you can see the reverse to be true, problem behavior that was not previously attached to an emotion when the behavior began, over time creates its own set of negative emotions. Clearly, there is an interplay that takes place between emotions and behavior.

## Behavior the Flip Side: Improving Yourself

There are positive behaviors that can help you solve problems, reduce emotional tension, and improve your life. To change, bad behavior needs to stop, and be replaced with new positive behavior. Remember the young man that returned the iPhone to the woman on the bus. His old behavior would have been to keep the iPhone. His new behavior was created by new thinking about how to treat others. This resulted in him returning the iPhone. If he continues to think and behave with regard toward others, his old behavior will truly have been replaced with new behavior.

To make improvements in your life means some behavior will have to stop. If you want to advance at work, but tend to be a bit lazy, or a work procrastinator, this will have to stop. At the same time, there will be things you need to start to do, like learning new job skills. This same thing is true when it comes to good health.

Take two people who are developing health problems that need to be addressed. One person chooses to start going to the gym after work instead of having a few drinks with his friends. He becomes aware that sitting at his desk all day is having negative consequences on his health. Are you aware that sitting at your desk at work all day is considered a health risk, the new smoking?

The second man is overweight and is beginning to experience the same health problems. There is the positive behavior he will need to start doing and the negative behavior he will need to stop doing. But he may not yet be ready to make changes in his life, or he may have a negative attitude about making those changes. As you look at both men's responses, their thinking leads them to the decision they will make about what they are going to do, or not do.

## Behavior: What Motivates Us

Behavior is goal-driven. The goal motivates us to behave in certain ways to achieve what we want. Most of the time we are not conscious we are reaching for a goal. So many of the things we do each day are small and inconsequential. They do not take much conscious thought to make happen. When you are hungry your goal is to satisfy your hunger. When you are tired it is time to get sleep. These two things do not take a lot of thinking to reach the goal of satisfying your hunger or needing sleep. Life is filled with these types of small goals each day. There may be different options available in how to reach that goal, but they all end with the same result, obtaining the goal.

Many of the small goals you achieve throughout each day take place without much effort. There is not a lot of conscious thinking that goes into reaching these goals. If you were having to consciously think about why you do everything you do by analyzing each choice you make, you would go nuts.

In taking a look at how this plays out in a morning routine, most people pretty much sleepwalk through the same routine each day to prepare for work. There are things you know you must do each day with some modest changes here and there. When the weekend comes most people have a different morning routine.

The big goal each morning is to get ready for work. Each behavior in your routine works to accomplish this goal. There are individual behaviors that must be done to reach the bigger goal of getting ready for work. Each of these individual behaviors has a goal too. The reason you take a shower, brush your teeth, and choose the clothes you wear. Each has a purpose in how and why you do them. Each smaller behavior fits into accomplishing the bigger goal of getting ready for work. These behaviors are goal-driven.

Once you understand that your behavior has a purpose, a goal to be reached, it can become easier to find out what the goal of your problem behavior is. When you understand the goal behind your bad behavior, you can then search for healthy and appropriate ways to reach that goal. Motivation is what drives your behavior and influences the choices you make to reach your goal.

Learning an adolescent's motivation behind their behavior had a lot to do in my court evaluations. I interviewed two different youth who had been arrested for stealing. The first youth had stolen a new pair of tennis shoes. When asked why he had done this he replied, "School was starting, and my mother had no money for new shoes for school." I verified this with his mother. You can at least sympathize with this youth without condoning the behavior. His motivation was clear.

The second youth when questioned replied, he did it for the excitement of stealing. He would get an adrenaline rush when he stole things. He told me he gave away the things he stole because he did not want them. His motivation was clear. Same behavior—stealing—but there was a totally different motivation for why they stole things. Once you are aware of the motivation for your bad behavior, you can find new behavior to replace the old behavior. Helping the first youth get a job could help him get what he needed and prevent him from coming back to probation.

## Behavioral and Classical Conditioning

Pavlov's experiment showed how a neutral object combined with a specific behavior could cause a change in the dog's behavior. Classical conditioning can be seen in problem behaviors, as well as in addictive behavior. A kitchen spoon can become the stimulus for a heroin addict to want to use again. The spoon can trigger a past memory of drug use, just like the bell caused the dog to salivate. This memory creates a psychological desire and physiological urge to use heroin, even when there is no heroin in sight.

This same type of thing happened in Pavlov's dog when it salivated to the bell, but there was no food was in sight. The dog's brain was triggered by the bell in the same way a drug user's brain triggers a desire to use drugs. To break an addiction a person will have to disconnect from the things that trigger their past behavior, disconnecting it from an urge to use in the present.

Classical conditioning can be seen in an anxiety reaction. Two people enter a crowded mall to shop. One person continues to walk forward while the other person becomes aware of a rapid rise in their heart rate. Quickly this person realizes they are having a panic attack. Their only thought now is to get out of the store. Their anxiety was triggered by thoughts and feelings that came with it as they entered the crowded mall. No matter what caused the thought, their response is no different from the dog's response to the ringing bell. Anxiety is a conditioned response triggered by a thought, connected to a stimulus in the environment.

## Operant Conditioning

B.F. Skinner focused on Operant Conditioning, meaning behavior that can be *reinforced* through *reward*, or *extinguished* by *punishment*. Operant conditioning can be seen at work in many aspects of our daily lives. I experienced a few episodes of operant conditioning growing up when I visited the principal's office for my bad behavior. Back then they had a paddle they could use to help correct bad behavior and encourage better behavior in the future.

Correctional institutions are built on Operant Conditioning, punishing bad behavior with the hope of extinguishing a person's criminal behavior. It may work for some, but not for others. Getting a paycheck should be considered a reward for working. The paycheck hopefully reinforces a desire to continue to work in the future.

For some, a paycheck may not be enough motivation to want to work. I have seen people who choose to remain unemployed and engage in panhandling or criminal behavior to get what they want, instead of earning the money by working. One of the things that helped many of the kids on probation to stop delinquent behavior was getting a job. This resulted in their lives changing for the better, getting off probation quicker, and less likely to return. Once they learned they could earn money to buy things by working, they quit stealing, and many of them quit using drugs. Replacing bad behavior with good behavior produced positive results.

Operant conditioning falls short in its ability to explain why positive reinforcement or negative punishment does not work at times for some people. While some probation youth I worked with found that their punishment was enough to change their behavior for the better, others did not. If their behavior did not change some of these kids were headed to higher levels in the juvenile system and graduating to the adult system.

The fundamental principle behind operant conditioning is solid and does have an application to how we live. But a person's motivation, the goal behind their behavior, can override the effects of reward and punishment. Therefore, a person can continue to make the same mistakes and suffer the same consequences, despite being offered a reward to change, or punishment to stop what they are doing.

- Behavior can be conditioned. You can see the effects of conditioned behavior in both problem and addictive behavior.
- Behavior can be reinforced or extinguished.
- Rewards for good behavior, and punishment for bad behavior, can be neutralized by a goal that overrides the intended effects of reward and punishment.

- Behavior is repetitive.
- Behavior is goal-driven, whether consciously or unconsciously.
- Behavior is always the result of how we think.

*"If you can change your mind, you can change your life."*
-William James

I repeatedly taught probation youth I worked with that they always had more than one choice. This is important because most of these kids did not see any other choices they could have made when they committed the crime. This exemplifies the tunnel vision that develops in drug addiction, criminal behavior, and crisis situations.

There is always more than one choice, but many of these kids could not figure that out. Some of them did not care that there was a second choice they could make. They were going to do what they wanted anyway. You always have more than one choice, even when the second choice is not attractive.

In the Commitment to Change video series, a criminal who is currently in prison talks about robbing a convenience store. He reports he points a gun at the young female sales clerk behind the counter and tells her he wants the money. He reports that the young clerk looks at him and then closes the safe. This leaves him with a choice, to shoot the girl because she closed the safe, or to leave the store without shooting her. He chooses to leave and not shoot her. (5)

The young girl had at least two choices—give him the money, or do not give him the money and risk being shot. The problem for most of us is that we do not see the second choice as a choice. Even when a gun is pointed at you, there are still at least two choices.

## Why Is This Important to Know?

When a person feels like they only have one choice, this can lead to a feeling of powerlessness. There is no other choice, but this one thing only. I must do it. Feeling powerless by not having other options can lead to some powerful negative emotions. Having more than one choice empowers you. Having many choices is even better.

Can you think of another choice she could have made? She could have tried to talk him out of committing the robbery. It does not matter what you think the outcome of that conversation would be, you are simply looking for as many possible choices you can come up with to solve the problem.

There was a story in the newspaper of a woman who was held at gunpoint and about to be raped. This lady chose to begin a conversation with the would-be rapist. The woman was a Christian and began to talk to the man about his life and whether he believed in God. After a long conversation, the man chose to let her go unharmed. What would you have done?

Since much of our thinking and behavior has been conditioned by past experiences, it will take time to undo the conditioning.

## Competing Goals

Another obstacle to changing your life is competing goals. Think of this in terms of going out for dinner and having to choose which restaurant you want to go to. You have two favorite restaurants, one Italian and one Mexican. Both sound good, but you can only eat at one tonight. You must make a choice which one it will be? You think it over, sort out your options, and one will win out.

When you understand that you make choices like this based on the goal behind your behavior, you can start to look for positive ways to reach any goal in your life. For the youth who stole tennis shoes because there was no money for new ones, helping this youth get a job replaces their bad behavior going forward.

Although a person says they want to stop abusing drugs or alcohol, is their motivation to change greater than their desire to use? The competing goals of improving your life, versus getting high because you like the feeling that comes with this behavior, cannot be reached at the same time.

For every bad behavior you want to change, there is the competing goal of the new and positive behavior you want to replace it with. Your choice will be the result of which one you want more. This is no different from temptation. In temptation, there is doing the right thing versus the wrong thing. You cannot do both. You either give in to the temptation or reject it.

Every person has the ability to make any choice in their life they want to make. Free will gives you the power of choice. Whether you struggle with an addiction, a specific repetitive problem behavior, or a mental health disorder, you have the ability to improve your life. The drug addict will continue to use, the alcoholic will continue to drink, and the criminal will continue to break the law until they make a decision that they want to change. This is as sure as the sun will rise tomorrow. There is no doctor, hospital, medication, prison, family member, or friend that can override a person's will. You will need to do that for yourself.

> *"We cannot solve our problems with the same thinking we used when we created them."*
> -Albert Einstein

## Back to the Consequences

You will never outrun the consequences of your bad behavior. Each one of us needs to firmly implant that into our thinking. I would tell the kids in my corrective thinking class that if they would stop for a minute and think about the consequences before they act in the future, that even if they choose to do the crime, they will have made progress because they actually thought it thru, even if they make the wrong choice. The reason I say this is that if they took the time to think about the potential consequences before acting, something they were not doing previously, then they had taken the first step in changing their behavior.

## Driving Under the Influence of Drugs or Alcohol

I was in a sandwich shop the other day talking with a young man who was taking my order. He mentioned that he was leaving work early because he had an appointment with his insurance provider. He said his insurance was going to increase due to two DUI's. I responded that I could understand the first DUI, but not the second one. I asked him what his thinking was when getting the second one. I heard the stock answer most of my probation kids tell me when they were caught breaking the law, "I don't know."

I told him, "That is not true; you were thinking something. Your brain never stops working when you are awake." He then admitted like many of my probation kids do, "I thought I would get away with it."

The problem behavior of drinking and driving was probably something he had done successfully numerous times in the past. We know the thinking behind his behavior, "I thought I would get away with it." What is missing in his thinking is the consequences of what could happen. These include being arrested, his car being towed, loss of his driver's license for a period of time, fines to pay, DUI classes to take, and counseling. There is also the consequence of the extra money he will have to pay in insurance for the next several years while the DUI is on his driving record. If he had thought of all those consequences before he drank and drove, he might have made a different choice? This young man may or may not drink and drive in the future. For now, he needs to think about what he has learned from this experience.

## Anger and Violence: A Deadly Partnership

I worked with a teenager fourteen years old who had been arrested for Battery with Substantial Bodily Harm. I tended to work with many violent youths during my time at juvenile court.

I found that he was a very angry kid. Underneath his anger, he was deeply hurt. Not knowing how to address his emotional pain he used anger and aggression to cover it up. The anger was due to his father being in prison. He felt his father had deserted his family, leaving the family in a difficult situation. He was aware of the undue stress this created for his mother who had to cover all the responsibilities at home. It was amazing how many times this same scenario played out in the adolescents I worked with.

He was an intelligent and insightful kid, which helped him realize that his behavior, lashing out at others, was because of the anger he felt toward his father. Since he could not take his anger out on his father, he had to find someone or something he could take it out on. Believe it or not, he did not see that harming others was wrong. The kid he attacked had done nothing to him and had nothing to do with his anger at his father. The other kid was simply an outlet for his anger.

Through counseling, he was able to redirect his anger back toward his father, the person he needed to address to resolve his anger. We talked about some things he could do to express his anger appropriately including writing a letter to his father in prison. This would allow him to release his anger in an appropriate way.

By the time we were done with counseling, he had come to the point that he felt real remorse for his victim. He was encouraged to get away from the friends that encouraged his violent behavior. This may be true for you too. In making changes in your life some of you may need to get away from the negative influences in your life whether family or friends.

*Brad Garrett*

# Drinking Instead of Dealing with the Problem

One person I counseled had developed a drinking problem following his divorce. The divorce had caught him off guard, and as a result, he had developed some mild anxiety. Although he was a social drinker previously, he was not a daily drinker.

When he would get off of work, he would stop by a certain liquor store to buy a bottle of wine on the way home. Once home he would drink until going to bed. After about three to four months of this, he recognized this was not a good way to deal with his divorce and sought help.

We talked about how his anxiety was a temporary reaction to the divorce. I felt he could resolve his current feelings of anxiety without medication since his anxiety was a recent development, and his anxiety level was a four to five, with no history of anxiousness in the past. His anxiety revolved around going to an empty home.

The first thing we did was to normalize his anxiety by seeing it was a normal response another person might have in his circumstance. We looked at ways he had handled stress in the past to help him see that he had solved stressful problems previously without alcohol.

His drinking began as a way to deal with his emotions caused by being alone after the divorce. His thinking led him to believe alcohol use was the best way to deal with the emptiness he felt and the anxiety that resulted.

Once he understood that the drinking interfered with his ability to deal with the anxiety, he knew he needed to stop drinking to address the real problem. Since his drinking pattern had recently developed, it only took a couple of sessions for him to break this pattern.

The day after making a decision to stop drinking, he said that as he was headed home from work, he felt a strong urge to buy alcohol. As he was nearing the turnoff for the liquor store he would go to, the urge to buy alcohol intensified. As the turnoff was now in front of him, he made a decision to use positive self-talk, telling himself that he did not need to drink tonight. He continued by telling himself he was strong enough to deal with the loneliness and anxiousness he might feel when he got home.

He said that as he drove past the turnoff, it was as if a weight lifted off him, the urge was gone, and he felt a sense of relief. The night went great he said. His anxiety continued for a few more days but was soon gone.

Sometimes the behavior we engage in to solve the problem can create a whole new set of problems you have to deal with.

- Changing behavior and breaking bad habits take a period of time to accomplish. Learning a new behavior and turning it into a positive habit is estimated to take about 30 days. That seems to be a little hopeful to me, but if it happens that quickly great. I believe that about two months, sixty days, is needed to entrench new behavior into a new habit.
- Bad habits, bad behavior, and uncontrolled emotions become wired into your brain's circuitry.
- The length of time needed to overcome a bad habit, at least in part, is based on the consistency of stopping your old behavior, followed by practicing the new behavior. The more consistent you are, the faster the bad habit is broken, and the new habit established.
- Even after establishing a new habit, you can slip back into old habit patterns momentarily. This occurs when you are in familiar circumstances and are not paying attention to what you are doing at the time. Suddenly you find yourself doing something automatically you had quit doing several weeks ago. There is no need to panic if this happens. Your brain is simply functioning in a familiar way that it has in the past due to your lack of focus. If this happens, simply return to your new thinking and practice the new behaviors to reinforce the changes you have made.

- The brain's circuitry is one of the reasons that addicts, as well as people who have deeply engrained behavior problems relapse. The brain's circuitry becomes hardwired due to the lengthy period of time they have engaged in their addictive behavior. For addicts it is easier to return to old behavior than to make changes.

Change takes effort. To do the same thing over and over again takes no effort. If you have a long-established pattern of bad behavior you will need to be diligent in changing your thinking, keeping your emotions in check, and avoiding the friends that encourage a return to that behavior. No matter how bad the problem behavior is, you have the ability to change it. I know you can do this because I have worked with many people who have been set free from drug and alcohol addiction, repetitive criminal behavior, and have learned to control emotions that have gotten them in trouble in the past.

# Reprogram Your Brain

*"I've got the brain of a four-year-old. I'll
bet he was glad to be rid of it".*
-Groucho Marx

We now come to the final step in learning how to control your emotions and change your behavior by reprogramming your brain. If you started to apply what you have learned in the earlier chapters, you have already started the process of making changes to your brain believe it or not.

I want to take the keep it simple stupid approach to the brain. This is the same approach I used when we looked at the health problems caused by high-energy negative emotions. This chapter is not meant to be a comprehensive look at the brain and how it works. I am not a brain expert, but I do know some things about how it functions.

## Amygdala and an Emotional Response

You have learned that the initial physiological response kicks in simultaneously with the emotional response, which leads to a programmed behavioral response. These programmed responses are generated by the brain, the amygdala. But how does the amygdala decide whether a stimulus will lead to an emotional reaction? Because sometimes it doesn't.

The amygdala operates from implicit memories. Implicit memories are emotional memories from past experiences. Your past emotional experiences are stored in the amygdala's memory bank. These emotional memories contribute to what you are feeling in the present.

The amygdala also contains repetitive memories such as how to ride a bike. Once you learned how to ride a bike, this information is secured in the amygdala memory bank. The next time you want to perform this task, you can do it with minimal conscious effort. Implicit memories work at a non-conscious level, meaning you may not be aware of them. But they are ready to be pulled up the next time you want to ride a bike, shoot a basketball, or go swimming as an example, you do not have to learn them all over.

Your emotional memories play a role in how the amygdala interprets what just happened to you, the stimulus. These emotional memories become wired into the amygdala leading to how it will respond. We have seen this at work in fight-or-flight, and emotions are no different.

These emotional memories play a big role in people who suffer from Post-Traumatic Stress Disorder (PTSD). Past traumatic experiences can become hardwired in the brain, making it difficult—not impossible—to establish new pathways in the brain.

There are both good and bad emotional memories stored in the amygdala. These memories do not have to be consciously thought about to trigger a current emotional response. The present situation does not have to be the same as a past situation to trigger a response, it only needs to be similar in some way to the past experience. Once triggered, an emotional response occurs.

For people with PTSD, the triggering of their past memories can lead to an emotional crisis. When this happens, the amygdala is responding to a past memory in the present moment. Remember that the present situation only has to be similar to a past memory, not the same.

Take touching a hot stove as an example. A burnt finger is filed away as a memory. The next time you get near a hot stove your brain will send a signal telling you not to touch the stove. You may not even recall the memory of the hot stove from the past, but you are aware not to touch the stove.

What you want to happen is expand this knowledge, touching the hot stove, by generalizing this information to other things that are hot. This same type of thing happens when an emotional reaction is generated in the present. It may not be the same person or situation from the past, but it is similar. We call this generalizing information to apply it in other situations.

## How Implicit Memories Work

Your implicit memories, like fight-or-flight, contribute to how you will behave in the future. The emotion you experienced in a past situation where you got angry or stressed creates a reference point in your memory. The amygdala develops a set of reference points to draw from when interpreting a new stimulus and determining what to do.

We learned the amygdala's functioning includes learning and memory. Learning and memory help in programming your future responses. Each time you respond in the same way, your emotional response is strengthened.

The ability to override your normal emotional-behavioral response can be seen in a person whose anger is controlled at work, but when they get home, it is a different matter. You do not yell at your boss, but you believe it is alright to yell at your spouse and kids. Thinking clearly precedes how a person behaves in both situations. Although the brain has been wired to respond in a certain way, under certain situations, the emotion can be controlled, and the behavior stopped or changed.

This provides insight into how to reprogram your responses; provide new information to your brain. A very simplistic way of reprogramming the amygdala is by telling yourself to stop, to stop responding in this way. In my speech presentation, I had to send the message to my brain to help me stop saying "you know" repeatedly. I learned how to drive stress-free by telling my brain not to respond to other drivers or react when red lights slowed me down. I needed to focus on the positive new things I can do. Focus on the music or scenery.

Because the amygdala works at a non-conscious level, it is easy to misunderstand why you just reacted the way you did. Most people are focused on what happened, not on their programmed response due to their thinking.

## A Memory and an Emotion

An example of an emotional memory happened as I was taking a lunch walk and listening to music on my iPod. A song by The Drifters began to play and immediately I was transported back to 14-years old and an eighth-grade pool party. I could remember some of the people who were there, especially one girl who liked me. With this memory came a happy, uplifting feeling. This past memory created positive feelings in the present. It felt good reflecting back on my adolescence, and might I say, innocence for a minute. This song came with an emotional memory attached to it. This memory had been stored away in my amygdala memory bank, waiting for an opportunity to be recalled.

A song can remind you of a really good time you had with a high school girlfriend or boyfriend. It can remind you of a relationship breakup. The song stimulates a memory that comes with an emotion. The emotion affects how you feel in the present, even if only temporarily. Attached to that past memory is all the thinking that surrounded the experience.

Let me share how a visual image can pull up a negative emotional memory. One young man in my anger management class was at a school bus stop when his friend was shot in a drive-by shooting. After the shooting, he had to wait for medical help for his friend who was bleeding, possibly dying. He did not, but a strong traumatic memory was set in place.

As a result, this teenager now avoids going near this bus stop. Why?

Because seeing the bus stop will cause him to relive the experience. The bus stop triggers an emotional memory, not just the details of what happened there, but the emotions that went with it. I have worked with several kids who have had similar experiences.

Trauma memories can come from experiences like war, rape, molestation, a threat to life, watching a violent crime take place, or a person's death. My friend was traumatized by a scary Twilight Zone episode and will not watch anything that is scary.

These experiences are imprinted into the amygdala's emotional memory bank. These memories can come with some very powerful visual images. These images can form the basis for nightmares or daymares. A daymare is when these images are pulled up while you are awake. This can happen when a person has to give an account of something that happened to them or they saw happen to another person. It can be a terrifying experience.

You had better believe that the adolescent who witnessed his friend being shot, and the blood that came with it, created very powerful negative emotions and strong visual images. The point here is that whether it is a good or bad emotional memory, an emotion felt in the present time, can be triggered by a past event.

## Reprogram Your Brain's Response to the Stimulus

Reprogramming your brain can be likened to reshaping your body. They both require an intentional effort to make it happen. It will not happen naturally. Getting fat seems to! The effort required to reprogram your brain will need to continue day-by-day, I use sixty days, to lock in place new thinking and behavior.

The amount of time needed to rewire your brain is an individual issue influenced by different factors. One of the biggest factors is based on how deeply engrained the negative thinking and behavior is. A second factor is effort, and a third is consistency.

To retrain the amygdala not to react, you need to consciously send messages to yourself/your brain, you want to make changes. You will need to stay aware of your thinking in the present moment, so you do not fall back into default mode, repeating the same old thing. From here you continue to practice your new thinking, every day until it becomes your natural way of thinking.

Most of the fears people have were created by a past experience. One example of how fear can be created is by getting thrown off of a horse. If a person gets bucked off a horse, do they get right back on before their fear takes hold? Or. do they become afraid it will happen again? If their fear forms, they may never get on a horse again.

An unusual way for a fear to develop is by watching a movie like Jaws. After watching Jaws many people developed a fear of swimming in the ocean. The fear was not based on a real experience of being confronted by a shark but an imagined fear created by what they just watched.

Anxiety is formed in this same way. It is based on an image of something that a person thinks will happen in the future. Whether it is a real personal experience or something that was created by imagination, the amygdala uses this information to program future responses.

Once the fear response is created, the amygdala is doing its job when a person sees the ocean and feels fearful. There might be a shark in there. To overcome the fear of wading into the ocean, much less swimming in it, means you need to confront the fear. The only way to do this is by changing your thinking behind your fear. Once that is done the ocean no longer creates an emotional fear reaction.

Reprogramming the amygdala will also stop the initial physiological response of the emotion. This is similar to extinguishing the dog's behavior of salivating to the bell.

A great way to reprogram your brain is by seeking out new information and having new learning experiences. The new information you gather, along with the new experiences you have, provides your brain with new material to draw from.

Positive self-talk is another technique for reprogramming your brain. Your brain will take your positive self-talk and go to work on eliminating the repetitious negative self-talk that has influenced your thinking, emotions, and behavior. Your brain is a powerful tool in the change process. Have confidence in your brain's ability to help you make those changes.

## Reprogramming Problem Behavior

Memories are important in forming behavior. Take riding a bicycle as an example of how implicit memory works in learning a repetitive behavior. Maybe you have not been on a bike for years. How long would it take for you to be able to ride a bike again?

When I go on vacation to Mission Beach in San Diego, one of the things I like to do is to rent a beach bike and ride along the path by the ocean. I do not ride a bike any other time during the year. However, I recently, during COVID, started riding my bike again. This was my way to deal with feeling locked in and my gym closed. It helped change my attitude by looking at positive things I could do for myself or be grumpy. Notice how I said "feeling locked-in," not being locked-in.

How long did it take for me to get on the bike and ride that first time? It was immediate. Did I have to consciously think about what I needed to do? Maybe for a few seconds at first, but then my brain kicked in and told my body what I needed to do. My stored memories of riding a bike as a kid was pulled up so that I could ride the bike in the present.

Once you have learned behavior, like riding a bike, implicit memories are created for future use. Each time you repeat a behavior you strengthen that behavior and reinforce the past memories that go with it. By riding a bike repeatedly, you became proficient at it. Soon you can ride the bike without a lot of conscious thought involved.

Your memories work in the same way with unproductive and problematic behavior. Once the bad behavior is formed, you do not have to spend time thinking about doing it in the future. Addictive behavior is programmed behavior that creates a neural pathway in your brain like a railroad track. The addiction creates an automatic response. It does not take much effort for the addiction to reoccur even after a period of abstinence. There is a saying that goes, if you always do what you have always done, you will always get what you always got. The path in the brain for bad behavior helps this happen.

Memories can be a good thing when the behavior serves a positive purpose like playing the guitar, driving a car, or riding a bike. Repetitious practice in forming a new behavior is important in solidifying the behavior.

Repetitious behavior becomes problematic when it becomes unproductive or destructive. It is interesting how addicts can selectively pull up the good thoughts that reinforce their addiction, but avoid the thoughts, like being arrested for drug use or a DUI that could discourage it.

## New Information and a New Perspective

A key to making changes in your life is by gathering new information. New information is needed to override old ways of thinking, false beliefs, unrealistic expectations, and distorted perceptions. It was the new information I received about my health from the Stress: Portrait of a Killer video that caused me to make changes in my life and write this book.

New information helps to give you a new perspective on how to live your life. When the teenagers I worked with learned they were not stuck with how they think, "I can get away with it," was replaced with "I don't want to be arrested again and put back on probation." This resulted in their life changing. They had learned how to rewire their brain by changing how they think.

I cannot stress enough the importance of educating yourself to improve yourself. For instance, if you want to learn more about how to eat better and live healthier to improve your brain, I recommend the book The Brain Fix by Ralph E. Carlson. If you want to learn more about anger or stress management, I recommend Anger Management for Dummies by W. Doyle Gentry, and Stress Management for Dummies by Allen Eiken. If you want to learn how to move forward in your life after suffering setbacks, I recommend Failing Forward by John Maxwell.

Educating yourself provides your brain with new resources to work with. New information is the difference between a professional who has all the knowledge, experience, and tools they need to do a job, versus you trying to do it yourself. There are a lot of things I can do, but after wrestling with trying to change out the walking belt on my treadmill, I finally gave up and asked a professional for help. By watching him I learned how to do it next time.

Learning new things provides you with new information to draw on to help you solve problems as they arise in the future. What you need to take from this chapter is how to use your brain to help you make the changes in your life you want.

# A Biblical Perspective: Spiritual Harmony

*"I will both lie down in peace and sleep;
For You alone are my safety."*
(Psalm 4:8)

How many people have problems with sleep? A lot. Do you? I know Christians that do. Yet God's word promises peace, safety, and sleep. If you have a problem sleeping, is it because of a health problem or due to pain that makes it difficult to sleep? Is it due to emotions such as stress, anger, and anxiety that keep your thoughts turned on?

Clinical depression can lead to sleep problems such as sleeping too much or not enough. For anyone who has experienced ongoing stress, you are aware of the difficulty of falling or staying asleep. When you finally did fall asleep, the stress was right there when you opened your eyes the next day. Did you know that a lack of sleep can actually increase emotional sensitivity and exacerbate mental health issues? Sleep should come naturally to us, but for some, it does not.

To combat the lack of sleep we have become a nation of pill takers. Some of the probation youth I worked with were prescribed Seroquel to help them sleep while they were stuck in detention or housed at Spring Mountain Youth Camp. Many of the kids I saw on probation smoked marijuana as a sleep aid.

If there is an indicator that a person is having some type of emotional or mental health problem in their life, it can be seen in how they are sleeping. It is recommended that adults get seven to nine hours of sleep a night for good brain health. How much do you get?

In Psalm 4:8 the writer says that he not only sleeps well, but he lies down in peace. Powerful negative emotions make it difficult to lie down in peace and sleep. One problem with negative emotions if you do not turn them off is not being to lie down in peace.

The Psalmist relates his ability of having good sleep to being at peace. His peace results from seeing God as his safety net. He trusts that God is watching over him as he sleeps, so his sleep is sound, restful. This shows he is in harmony with God and what your life and sleep should look like as a born-again believer.

## Back to the Garden

Life should be enjoyable, not stress-filled. There should be quality time spent with family and friends. There should be positive experiences of going places and doing things that are fun that will result in a treasure of positive emotions and good memories. When was the last time you felt nothing but good feelings and positive emotions for seven days without one negative emotion interfering? I meet and talk with many Christian people whose lives are filled with emotional turmoil, or who are struggling with mental health issues or bad behavior. This should not be how Christians live. God wants to bless you!

When your life is filled with negative emotions, they crowd out your ability to experience the positive ones, such as love, joy, peace, happiness, faith, contentment, and patience. These are all listed as fruit of the Spirit in Galatians 5:22-23. The result of getting your negative emotions under control will open the door to experiencing more of the positive emotions. Positive emotions help you to maintain a state of emotional balance, feel a greater sense of calm, create a mental state of well-being, and contribute to good brain health.

## Was It God's Intention for Man to Struggle with Negative Emotions?

No, and again I say no! God originally created man whole and complete. Adam and Eve lacked in no area of their life.

God gave Adam and Eve freedom of choice, what is referred to as free will. There appears to have been only one bad choice they could have made, which they did. This choice led to replacing man's perfection with imperfection.

We do not have any idea of how much time passed between the day Adam and Eve were created, to the day of their disobedience in the garden. We can assume that during this period of time, God's creation functioned in harmony as seen in man's relationship with Him, Adam and Eve's relationship with one another, and with nature. Once man fell, perfection ended, and harmony was lost. And our capacity for negative emotions was created.

## Negative Emotions Are a Product of Our Sinful Nature

God did not intend for man to go through life experiencing negative emotions. Think about this for a moment. If God considered His creation to be very good, then where would negative emotions like depression, anxiety, stress, and discouragement fit in? These emotions were not included as a part of the package when Adam was created.

Having a sinful nature does not rule out that you have the ability to do good, even kind things for others. A sinful nature does not take away your ability to care for and love others. Having a sinful nature means that you do not have the ability to restore your relationship with God, bring yourself back to the original state of perfection, or overcome your sinful tendencies by your own efforts. Your self-centered sinful nature is naturally inclined to reject God and His way.

Each one of us, before we committed our lives to Jesus, chose to travel down paths that were contrary to God's standard of living. "There is a way that seems right to a man, but its end is the way of death." (Proverbs 14:12.) The writer of Proverbs believes this message to be so important that he repeats it again in (Proverbs 16:25). If man's way leads to death, and man cannot restore himself to his original state, then who can do this?

## Perfection

Man's imperfections are continually seen in his fallen nature. These imperfections can be seen in his inability to control his emotions and in every type of bad behavior imaginable. Man's state of imperfection is seen in mental health issues and addiction. Two words—perfection and harmony—describe the Garden of Eden at creation.

The word *perfect* means that something is complete or whole. There is nothing that can be added to it that would make it better or improve it. When we say God is perfect, this means that there is nothing that can be added to God that would make Him more perfect or more complete. God is complete in Himself. He is in need of nothing. God is perfect, and therefore in perfect harmony within Himself.

God created us in His likeness and image. Therefore, man was created perfect, whole, and complete. This allowed man to live in a right relationship with God and with others. This all changed when man disobeyed God.

If man is going to be restored to his original state, only God who created man has the power to restore him. God is the only one who knows what man's original blueprint, his original state of perfection looks like. Although man fell in the garden, God had a plan for his restoration

Jesus speaks about God's ultimate desire for man in the Sermon on the Mount. "Therefore, you shall be perfect, just as your Father in heaven is perfect." (Matthew 5:48.) Jesus clearly instructs the crowd that it is God's desire for them to become perfect.

The Greek word used by Jesus for perfect is *teleios*, which means complete or a state of completeness. The word is in the future tense. Perfection, a state of wholeness and completion, will ultimately be accomplished at a future time. However, we are working on it now.

Paul, speaking about man's restoration says, "Him we preach, warning every man and teaching every man in all wisdom, that we may present every man perfect in Christ Jesus. (Colossians 1:28)" Paul identifies perfection as being completed at a future time. It was Paul who said in 2 Corinthians 5:17, "We are becoming a new creation."

For this to happen man will need something outside of himself to bring about this restoration. There are people who believe that man has the ability to do this for himself. He does not need God's help to do it for him. How foolish is this belief? The Bible paints an entirely different picture of man's ability to fix himself.

Only God has the ability to restore man to his original state. This can only happen through Jesus Christ and the work of the Holy Spirit in us.

"Jesus said to him, I am the way, the truth, and the life. No one comes to the Father except through me." (John 14:6.) The work of restoration begins with coming to the Father through Jesus Christ, His Son. It continues as the Holy Spirit works to transform us into Jesus image, true perfection

## Harmony

Harmony is a combination of musical notes to produce chords and chord progressions resulting in a pleasing sound. Harmony results when people combine their voices by singing in the same key resulting in a pleasing sound. Instruments are tuned to the same pitch so that when they are played, they are in harmony with other instruments. Harmony results in a pleasant sound. If an instrument is out of tune, it is not in harmony, and therefore produces an unpleasant sound.

An F note played on a guitar in Las Vegas will sound the same as one played on a guitar in New York. An F note can be played harmoniously with all other instruments playing the same note, whether it is a guitar, piano, or trumpet. Musical harmony is based on a universal pitch that is established for all instruments. A person cannot make up what an F note should sound like.

In like manner, man cannot determine what true completeness, wholeness, or harmony looks like in himself. Man does not have a true reference point, only God does. God is the universal measuring stick for determining what perfection and harmony look like. Because of this, He is the only one that can set the standard for how we are to behave and live.

To restore His work in us, God provided you with a helper, the Holy Spirit. Jesus said, "I will pray the Father, and He will give you another helper." (John 14:16) The word another in Greek means another of *the same kind*, meaning this helper is just like Jesus, *the same kind*.

The work of restoration begins with repentance and receiving Jesus as your savior. It continues by establishing a daily relationship with God through prayer and reading God's word. It continues daily by being open to the ongoing work of the Holy Spirit in you.

## The Need to Change Behavior

God sets the standard for man's behavior in the Old Testament book of Exodus. The Ten Commandments are the basics for how God expects us to live. We need to recognize that the Ten Commandments are not the ten suggestions. A commandment is written or spoken in the imperative mood. This can be seen in phrases like "shut the door," "clean your room," and "be at work on time." These are not simple requests; they are commands telling someone what to do. The Ten Commandments are written in the imperative mood and are telling us how to live.

Many of the scriptures we read in the New Testament are commands too, written in the imperative mood. New Testament commands reveal how we are to live and behave. They are no different from the Ten Commandments and how God expected the Israelites to live and behave.

Jesus in the Sermon on the Mount references the seventh commandment regarding adultery. "You have heard that it was said to those of old, You shall not commit adultery. But I say to you that whoever looks at a woman to lust for her has already committed adultery with her in his heart. (Matthew 5:27-28)"

Jesus not only reinforces the seventh commandment; He also raises the bar to the next level for how His followers are to live. Jesus equates looking at a woman lustfully as being on the same level as committing adultery. Why? Because Jesus looks at the heart, not just the behavior. The New Testament is filled with various commands regarding how we are to live and behave, which will reveal your heart condition and your willingness to obey by making changes.

If a person calls themselves a Christian and lies to others, the ninth commandment, or steals from others, the eighth commandment, then their behavior is not in line with what God has told us about how we are to live. Whether a commandment is in the Old or New Testament, a commandment is still a commandment, setting basic requirements for Christian living.

Whereas the need to control and change behavior for a non-Christian is a choice, for a Christian it is a command that dictates how you are to live "Therefore, putting away lying, let each one of you speak truth with his neighbor . . ." (Ephesians 4:25.) "Let him who stole steal no longer, but rather let him labor, working with his hands what is good, that he may have something to give him who has need." (Ephesians 4:28.) Both these NT commandments dictate behavior to stop and behavior to start.

We are to stop the bad behavior first, followed by replacing it with positive behavior. The positive behavior Paul refers to includes speaking the truth, working with your own hands, and giving to him who is in need.

In spite of the command not to commit adultery, how many Christian marriages and Christian ministries have been ruined by a person's disobedience to this command. You cannot tell me these people did not know that adultery was wrong. But like Adam and Eve, every person has been given free will to choose at any time to go God's way or their own way. However, consequences will follow.

Let us look at the importance the Bible places on another behavior, how we talk. "Let no corrupt word proceed out of your mouth, but what is good for necessary edification, that it may impart grace to the hearers." (Ephesians 4:29.) In this verse, we see the old behavior we are to stop, corrupt communication. We are to exchange it with new behavior, speaking what is good to build others up.

How many of you are aware that the Bible commands you to control how you talk? Colossians expands on the issue of how you talk by stating that we are to put away, "... filthy language out of our mouth." (Colossians 3:8.) You can interpret what filthy language means for yourself, for me it meant to quit cussing. I still remember when God began to deal with me about my need to clean up my vocabulary. The Bible sets a high standard for Christian behavior, including how we talk.

Every command presents a choice for what you will choose to do. Everyone who calls themselves a Christian believer is given choices every day as to whether they will follow the Biblical guidelines for their behavior and emotions or go it on their own.

## The Need to Control Emotions

### Anger

The Bible is clear that Christians have a responsibility to control their emotions. When was the last time you heard a sermon on the need to control your emotions? Unfortunately, many Christians miss the importance the Bible places on controlling their emotions. There is far more awareness about the need to change bad behavior than there is to control your emotions.

In the Sermon on the Mount, Jesus addresses the issue of anger. "But I say to you that whoever is angry without cause with your brother is in danger of judgment." (Matthew 5:21-22.) The words "without cause" have been left out in some translations of the New Testament because it muddies the water as to what would be legitimate reasons for anger. We saw in Genesis that Cain had no cause to be angry at his brother, and yet Cain's anger led him to kill his brother.

Paul addresses the need to control anger in Ephesians. "Be angry and do not sin do not let the sun go down on your wrath." (Ephesians 4:26.) The words "be angry" and "do not sin" were first recorded in (Psalm 4:4.)

"Cease from anger and forsake wrath; ..." (Psalm 37:8.) The word cease could also be translated as to let go of, or abandon. Make no mistake when reading these verses. They are commandments that tell us as Christians, we are to control, cease from, and let go of anger.

The importance of a Christian's need to control their anger or any other negative emotion is enhanced by being sandwiched between the two commandments regarding lying and stealing (Ephesians 4:25-30).

I want to leave you with three additional scriptures on anger without commentary from me.

- "A fool vents all his feelings, but a wise man holds them back." (Proverbs 29:11.)
- "Do not hasten in your spirit to be angry, for anger rests in the bosom of fools." (Ecclesiastes 7:9.)
- "So then, my beloved brethren, let every man be swift to hear, slow to speak, slow to wrath; for the wrath of man does not produce the righteousness of God." (James 1:19-20.)

I would like to add to this, three men who had difficulty controlling their anger at times.

- Moses (Exodus 32:19 and Numbers 20:11) is kept out of the Promised Land due to his anger causes him to disobey God (Numbers 20:7-12).
- King Saul's anger leads him to try to kill David, the future king (1 Samuel 18:7-12).
- King David's anger at Nabal leads to a desire to kill him, and if followed through, David would have been guilty of shedding innocent blood (1 Samuel 25:1-39).

Jesus's disciples, James and John, were given the name "sons of thunder" by Jesus. (Mark 3:17.) Although it is not specified as to what sons of thunder refers to, I lean toward the thought that these two brothers may have been hotheads. One indication of this is when they wanted to call fire down from heaven on a group of people because they refused to receive Jesus into their town. (Luke 9:51-56.)

## Worry and Stress

Next up is worry or stress, another emotion covered in the scriptures. I personally see the emotions of worry, stress, and anxiety as being on a continuum based on the level of energy each one generates. This is similar to the emotions of anger, irritation, and frustration, and the level of energy that comes with these closely related emotions.

Jesus addressed worry three times in the Sermon on the Mount. Each time he tells his followers that they are not to worry. Jesus is speaking in the imperative mood and repeats the command not to worry three times. The words worry and stress are interchangeable terms.

- "Therefore, I say to you, do not *worry* about your life, what you will eat, or what you will drink; nor about your body what you will put on . . ." (Matthew 6:25)
- "Therefore, do not *worry*, saying, what shall we eat? or What shall we drink? or What shall we wear?" (Matthew 6: 31)
- "Therefore, do not *worry* about tomorrow, for tomorrow will *worry* about its own things. Sufficient for the day is its own trouble" (Matthew 6:34)

Jesus is commanding the people not to worry about food, drink, and clothing, the basics of life. He tells them not to worry about what might happen tomorrow. A command not to worry is pretty strong language. How can Jesus command you not to worry? Worry is natural, isn't it? At least that is what most people believe. Jesus must not be aware of how difficult life can be.

Jesus challenges their thinking about life and worry by asking a question. "... Is not life more than food, and the body more than clothing?" (Matthew 6:25)

Jesus challenges their thinking about God and their relationship with Him as their Heavenly Father. He uses the birds to show how God provides, indicating God will provide for them. "... Are you not of more value than they?" (Matthew 6:26). The answer is yes.

Jesus encourages them by saying, "For your heavenly Father knows that you need all these things." (Matthew 6:32) The implication is clear. God knows you and what you need as His child. He will meet those needs. One of the names of God in the Old Testament is Jehovah-Jireh, "the Lord will provide" (Genesis 22:14).

Jesus links worry to a lack of faith. "O, you of little faith." (Matthew 6:30). He addresses the real issue behind fear and anxiety—a lack of faith. A friend of mind, after talking together, realized her anxiety was caused by a lack of faith at times due to how she had been conditioned to respond in a crisis. She learned to replace the anxiety with prayer, which increased her trust in God and overcome the anxiety.

Jesus links worry to thinking about the future. "Therefore, do not worry about tomorrow . . ." (Matthew 6:34). The biggest contributor to worry, stress, and anxiety is thinking about what could come. Jesus's answer to worry about the future is let go and focus on today.

Jesus challenges their thinking about anxiety. "Which of you by worrying can add one cubit to his stature?" (Matthew 6:27). Does being anxious, worried, or stressed change one thing? No! But it creates a lot of unwanted problems.

Jesus is telling the people that they need to change how they think about their daily life and God's participation in it as their heavenly Father and provider. He wants the people to refocus from their needs, to seeing God is their provider. Faith in God overcomes worry, stress, and anxiety.

*You can replace your worry with faith
by seeing how great God is.*

I want to follow Jesus's words with the words of Paul in the book of Philippians. "Be anxious for nothing, but in everything by prayer and supplication, with thanksgiving, let your request be made known to God; and the peace of God which surpasses all understanding will guard your hearts and minds through Christ Jesus." (Philippians 4:6-7.)

Paul uses the same Greek word translated in Philippians as anxiousness that Jesus used for worry in Matthew. The Greek word translated as anxious or worry in both texts can be defined as to be divided, distracted, or split in parts. This conveys the thought that when a person is anxious, they have become split apart or divided in their thinking and emotions, causing them to become distracted and lose focus.

Anxiety is defined as a state of heightened mental and emotional tension, a feeling of apprehension. Anxiety is negative energy rooted in fear. Anxiety is felt when a person senses a loss of control, or when there is an inability to predict a future outcome of something that will have an effect on them. Anxiety is a perfect example of man's loss of harmony within himself. There is no peace with anxiousness, worry, or stress. You cannot experience these types of negative emotions and be at peace within yourself.

Paul clearly provides an answer for anxiety. It is to call upon God in prayer, with thanksgiving, mixed together with faith. As a result, God gives you His peace. God guards your heart and mind keeping away the negative thoughts and emotions that lead to anxiousness.

God not only commands us not to be anxious, but He also provides the way to live above anxiousness. This is clearly an indication that God does not want you to struggle with negative emotions including stress, anxiety, anger, and depression. His will for you is to live in peace, with a peace that surpasses all understanding.

Jesus said to his followers, "Peace I leave with you, my peace I give to you; not as the world gives, do I give to you. Let not your heart be troubled, neither let it be afraid." (John 14:27.) Are you living in the peace that Jesus gives to us? If not, why not?

The Greek word for anxious can also be translated as "cares" or "cares of this world." The word *cares* relates to life in general and the problems that come with life, which can lead to anxiousness. Jesus clearly does not want you to worry or be anxious. God is with you.

I will leave you with three verses and one New Testament story on worry, stress, and anxiety.

- "Search me, o God, and know my heart; Try me and know my anxieties." (Psalm 139:23.)
- Jesus speaking to his followers tells them, "But take heed to yourselves, lest your hearts be weighed down with carousing, drunkenness, and cares of this life, and that Day come on you unexpectedly." (Luke 21:34.) The word cares could be replaced with the word stress or anxiety.
- "Casting all your care upon Him, for He cares for you." (1 Peter 5:7.) Peter tells you how to resolve the worry, stress, and anxiety that comes with life. Put it all on Jesus's shoulders to carry. The word picture that comes with this scripture is of a person who is carrying a heavy load on their shoulders. Jesus comes along and offers to carry it for them.

Mary and Martha, two sisters, are having Jesus and his disciples over for dinner. Mary is sitting at the feet of Jesus listening to him speak, while Martha is working in the kitchen. Martha becomes unhappy with her sister's lack of help, so she addresses her concerns with Jesus. "And Jesus answered and said to her, Martha, Martha, you are worried and troubled about many things. But one thing is needed, and Mary has chosen that good part, which will not be taken from her." (Luke 10:41-42.)

- Jesus tells Martha that she is worried and troubled about many things.
- Her busyness has caused her to miss the most important thing; sitting at Jesus's feet listening to him teach. Her priorities are confused as to what is important in life.
- This story is an example of how busyness, even important busyness, and the normal cares of life can grow anxieties and stress that choke out spiritual things. How about you? Are your cares of life keeping you from sitting at Jesus's feet each day to receive the spiritual blessing he wants to pour out on you?

## Depression

The word depression is not a common term used in the Bible. That does not mean that people did not get depressed in the Old or New Testament. There are other terms that are used that convey the same idea as depression.

"Anxiety in the heart of man causes depression …" (Proverbs 12:25.) The Hebrew word translated as depression can be translated as to make stoop, or to weigh down. Depression weighs people down. The burden of depression makes it difficult for people to get through each day. It feels as if something is pressing down on them, weighing them down.

"Hope deferred makes the heart sick …" (Proverbs 13:12.) The word *sick* can be translated as weak; to suffer or grieve. A loss of hope is clearly linked with depression. Coupled with a loss of hope is a feeling of helplessness. There is nothing I can do to change this.

"A merry heart makes a cheerful countenance, but by sorrow of the heart the spirit is broken." (Proverbs 15:13.) This is one of the clearest pictures of what depression looks like. People who are clinically depressed are broken inside. It is like a fracture of the soul that has taken place within them. Depression becomes more about surviving each day than living each day.

"A merry heart does good like medicine, but a broken spirit dries the bones." (Proverbs 17:22.) Depression breaks a man's spirit. Dries the bones can be a metaphor for the fatigue that depression brings with it. The Bible's medication is a cheerful heart.

I want to close this section on depression with two verses in Psalms.

The first one is, "Save me O God! For the waters have come up to my neck. I sink in deep mire, where there is no standing: I have come into deep waters, Where the floods overflow me. I am weary with my crying; My throat is dry; My eyes fail while I wait for my God." (Psalm 69:1-3.)

"I am troubled, I am bowed down greatly; I go mourning all day long. For my loins are full of inflammation, and there is no soundness in my flesh. I am feeble and severely broken. I groan because of the turmoil of my heart." (Psalm 38:6-8.)

These two psalms are painting a person who is in deep distress, what would be identified as depression. David's answer to his depressed condition and brokenness was to cry out to God for help and deliverance from his condition. David continually put his trust in God and held on to God's promises of deliverance, healing, and blessing. "I sought the Lord and He heard me, and He delivered me from all my fears." (Psalm 34:4.). This is no different for you as a Christian.

Depression is a treatable disorder that can be overcome without medication. However, if you are on medication, continue to take your medication and work with your doctor. Then use what you have learned in this book to improve your thinking about the things that tend to make you depressed. Above all exercise your faith in Jesus and be open to the Holy Spirit's work in you. We will talk about low-energy emotions and depression in the next chapter.

More than that though, cry out to God for help and ask Him to heal you. Exercise the faith God has given you and put your trust in Him as your heavenly Father.

## The Holy Spirit: Your Helper

God has laid out his expectations for how Christians are to live. Although he sets a high standard of behavior that seems impossible to reach, He provides us with a helper to accomplish this in us. We have not been left to our own devices to try to change ourselves.

Jesus said as he was nearing the end of his earthly ministry, "And I will pray the Father, and He will give you another Helper, that He may abide with you forever, the Spirit of truth, whom the world cannot receive because it neither sees Him nor knows Him;

but you know Him for He dwells with you and will be in you." (John 14:16-17.) The Christian life begins with the new birth, the result of being born of God by the Holy Spirit. The new birth results in the Holy Spirit taking up residence in your heart.

Although the Bible sets a high standard for how we are to live, God gives us the Holy Spirit to accomplish the work in us. "…work out your own salvation with fear and trembling; for it is God who works in you both to will and to do for His good pleasure." (Philippians 2:12-13.) Paul points out that the work of salvation is a choice of your free will that allows the Holy Spirit to work in you as it pleases God. The Holy Spirit helps you overcome your sinful nature, your bad choices, and bad behavior. Your job is to allow Him to do the work in you.

God has provided His Word, the Bible to reveal Himself to us. The Bible teaches us what God is like and how we are to live in a relationship with Him. This includes daily reading His word, prayer, and thanksgiving. What I have provided in the other chapters of this book is an understanding of how emotions work within us as humans, and to give you the tools you need to control and change them, as well as change problem behavior. In addition to those tools, you have been given the power of the Holy Spirit to help you change everything about you that you are willing to allow God to change in you.

## Last Words on Emotions

God not only wants us to overcome our negative emotions, but He also wants us to be filled with all the positive ones. I want to leave you a few verses to show you what He wants to give you.

"But the fruit of the Spirit is love, joy, peace, longsuffering, kindness, goodness, faithfulness, gentleness, self-control…" (Galatians 5:22-23.)

"… Do not sorrow, for the joy of the Lord is your strength." (Nehemiah 8:10.)

"Rejoice in the Lord always. And again, I will say, rejoice." (Philippians 4:4.)

"You have turned for me my mourning into dancing; You have put off my sackcloth and clothed me with gladness," (Psalm 30:11.)

"The Lord will give strength to his people; The Lord will bless his people with peace. (Psalm 29:11.)

I decided to leave you with these verses without any commentary so that you could meditate upon them for yourself to see how they apply in your life. The Bible is filled with references to emotions, both positive and negative. It is also filled with stories of people and their bad behavior. I wish I had the time to go through some of those stories and expand on them with you, but that will have to be for another time and place. The Bible is filled with the hope that God is greater than our problems.

I want to close this chapter with Paul's benediction to the Corinthians. "Finally, brethren, farewell. Become complete. Be of good comfort, be of one mind, live in peace; and the God of love and peace will be with you." (II Corinthians 13:11.) Amen.

# Low-Energy Negative Emotions

*"I, not events, have the power to make me happy or unhappy today. I can choose which it shall be. Yesterday is dead, tomorrow hasn't arrived yet. I have just one day, today, and I'm going to be happy in it."*
-Groucho Marx

## Brain and Body
## Emotions> I-------------v-------------I <Behavior
## Neurotransmitters

You were introduced to the concept of the emotional barbell in chapter six as a way to visualize the interaction between the various components involved in creating an emotional reaction. In the diagram above the only change that has been made is replacing adrenaline and cortisol with neurotransmitters. A neurotransmitter is a chemical substance responsible for good brain health, as well as your overall level of functioning. The three main neurotransmitters are dopamine, serotonin, and epinephrine.

The human brain contains billions of nerve cells called neurons. These nerve cells communicate with one another through electrical and chemical signals that play out in our thinking, behavior, and emotions. These neurons communicate through the release of chemicals, creating electrical impulses.

There is a small gap between one neuron and the next neuron in line. One neuron communicates with the next neuron through the release of neurotransmitters. The communication between neurons works on a catch and pass basis, similar to a baseball pitcher and catcher. One neuron is the pitcher. The next neuron is the catcher. The neurotransmitter is the ball they are passing.

The first neuron, the pitcher, releases these chemicals, which are then caught by the catcher who represents the next neuron in line. This neuron has receptor sites that are able to receive the chemical transmission from the first neuron. The receiving neuron becomes the new pitcher who passes the ball onto the next new neuron.

Neurotransmitters link our brain with our body. Neurotransmitters have an impact on our mental and emotional health. When the release and catch communication between neurons works properly, everything works great and we feel great. When the transmissions break down various mental health issues can develop. When this happens, medication is usually prescribed to repair the connection.

Low-energy negative emotions are the result of an interruption in the functioning of the communication between neurons. When this communication system breaks down there may be a need for medication, at least temporarily. But medication is not always needed to resolve the issue. In some instances, proper nutrition and exercise can help restore the system.

## Defining Low-Energy Negative Emotions

Low-energy negative emotions can suck the life out of you like a vampire sucks the life out of a person by draining their blood. These emotions can start as a slow leak in a tire. If not caught in time these emotions can flatten you like a flat tire. At other times these emotions can result from being hit by a circumstantial tidal wave of problems such as the death of someone close, or a health crisis. When this happens, you feel the full force of the wave in your emotions. With these emotions, you will need to remind yourself that all emotions begin as a reaction to a stimulus.

The difference between high-energy versus low-energy emotions is that one is like grabbing a live wire, while the other is subtle and sneaks up on you. The initial reaction that comes with low-energy emotions is like letting air out of a tire. The full weight of these emotions may not settle in for a period of time after the incident occurs.

Low-energy negative emotions drain your physical, emotional, and mental energy similar to the effect of leaving the lights on your car. It drains the battery. Low-energy emotions drain the brain.

Sometimes these low-energy emotions can be covered over by a high-energy emotion like anger, temporarily though. When someone does something that hurts you, instead of dealing with the hurt, you respond with anger. The anger resulted from being hurt. Anger is a symptom of being hurt. When you resolve the hurt, the anger is gone. Being hurt can lead to depression if not resolved.

## Characteristics of Low-Energy Emotions

You know from an earlier chapter that all emotions come with behavior that is congruent with the emotion. This is true for low-energy negative emotions. Emotions like depression drain your mental energy, which leads to a drain on your physical energy. The behavior is manifested in the things people stop doing that they used to do like spending time with friends, which is known as withdrawal. The way the person used to behave is replaced with negative behaviors that result from the low-energy emotion. Remember emotion and behavior are congruent with depression.

Many people who were very active before experiencing depression lose their interest in the things they once enjoyed doing. Losing interest in the things you once did, or not feeling pleasure when you do them are symptoms of depression. Because this change can be gradual, you may not recognize what is happening to you and the changes in your behavior.

Low-energy emotions do not only change a person's interest in doing things, they cause a person to *quit trying* to do things. With low-energy emotions, there is a tendency to *give in* to the negative thoughts or to the lack of energy that comes with depression.

What will be required to overcome depression is to fight against the tendencies and negative thinking that comes with depression. Depressed people tend to *quit doing* for themselves the very things they need to do to overcome the negative thoughts and lack of energy they feel.

Let us use a different low-energy emotion, discouragement, to look at the negative effect that comes with this emotion. You apply for a promotion at work, but someone who may be less qualified than you receives the promotion. As a result, you feel discouraged, which most people would. If this happens you have a couple of choices.

The first is to *give up* trying to be promoted in the future. The next time a promotion opens you talk yourself out of applying for it. The second option is to learn from the interview and experience, then take what you have learned into the next job interview. If you stay with the feeling of discouragement instead of learning from your experience you will become stuck.

A second thing that results from low-energy emotions is a thought to *withdraw* or *isolate*. With depression, a person may isolate from family and friends. This type of behavior is similar to people who feel physically sick. When a person is ill, they typically want to be left alone. When the person gets better, they begin to act like their old self. Low-energy negative emotions bring with them self-defeating behavior that reinforces the emotion. When one isolates from others it feeds and reinforces the depression.

Another behavior is *turning inward*. Turning inward leads to becoming focused solely on yourself in an extremely unhealthy way. Turning inward can be seen more clearly by others who know you than it is by yourself. You may think that what is happening in depression, discouragement, or disappointment is normal, but it is not. This is not how you felt or behaved before you felt depressed, disappointed, or discouraged.

The more you turn inward, the more your life changes in negative ways. Turning inward affects your relationship with others. When you turn inward, your thinking about others becomes distorted due to the negative focus that has developed in your life. This is similar to tunnel vision in high-energy emotions, but the narrowing of focus is on yourself, not the situation.

People with low-energy emotions can take on a *victim mentality*. Being a victim is dangerous because it leads to giving up your power to overcome what you are experiencing. Tunnel vision causes you to lose perspective of the world around you. You lose sight of how to solve the problem. You become a prisoner of the emotion. The more a person engages in the emotional thinking, and behavior that comes with it, the more it reinforces the emotion.

Over time the emotion, thinking, and behavior become intertwined like a piece of rope. The person not only feels depressed, but they also look depressed, think depressed, and behave depressed. The more ingrained the low-energy emotion is, the greater the effort will be needed to overcome it, which is why medication may be needed. The pattern that has been habituated becomes their lifestyle. This is why a person who is clinically depressed needs help and may need to see a psychiatrist as quickly as possible to determine the need for medication.

A list of low-energy emotions includes loneliness, discouragement, disappointment, disillusionment, hurt, rejection, and abandonment. There are many others too. These powerful negative emotions have a dramatic negative effect on your life if you leave them unresolved.

A friend of mine dated a woman for a period of time whose husband had died two years earlier. He described how she had difficulty letting go of the loss of her husband. At times when things seemed to be going well in the relationship, she would pull back. After a time of isolating herself, she would initiate contact again.

There is no criticism intended for the women mentioned here. If you look at her behavior, it is congruent for a person who is still grieving from her loss. She is trying to move forward, but when something is triggered in her she pulls back. Low-energy emotions and behavior are congruent, predictable, and personalized like high-energy negative emotions.

## The Brain, Neurotransmitters, and Medication

When the normal flow of neurotransmitters is interrupted problems develop. One of our brain's responsibilities is to keep us in a state of good mental health. The neurotransmitters, dopamine, serotonin, and norepinephrine are responsible for good mental and emotional health. These chemicals keep our brains healthy and functioning properly.

When the neural connections break down, it is similar to a disease caused by a breakdown in the body's immune system. Sometimes medication may be needed to resolve these types of breakdowns. Sometimes these problems can be corrected through lifestyle changes.

It is normal to experience emotions like depression, discouragement, and disappointment at some time in life. Sometimes depression may be a case of the blues. The blues is considered situational depression caused by a recent problem or crisis. Situational depression tends to go away when the problem is resolved. Losing a job can lead to situational depression. Getting a new job resolves the depression. A relationship breakup can cause feelings of rejection. A new relationship makes them go away.

One problem with using psychotropic medication to address mental health concerns is similar to using medication to address a physical illness. If all you do is take the medication to address the problem, then you are failing to do for yourself the things you need to do. Medication should never be the only solution for low-energy emotions. Medication should be coupled with counseling, exercise, eating right, and controlling your thinking. All of these activities contribute to positive brain health.

The low energy that comes from these emotions is caused by the interruption of the neurotransmitters. Just as adrenaline increases your energy and leads to bad behavior, the breakdown of the neurotransmitters depletes your energy, leading to bad behavior.

A problem with low-energy emotions is that they cause you to feel like you do not have the energy you need to overcome them. Low-energy emotions can make it difficult to believe change is possible. This is why depression is called a "black hole," people cannot seem to have the energy to find their way out.

In working to overcome low-energy emotions look for a common theme, what is the thinking that may have caused it? If you have periods of depression, look for a theme. What is similar?

One theme that continually pops up with these low-energy emotions is feeling hurt. Hurt feelings are associated with abandonment, rejection, discouragement, and disappointment. To overcome these types of emotions you will need to address who or what has hurt you. You will need to forgive and then let go of the one who hurt, disappointed, rejected, or abandoned you. Once you let go of the person who hurt you, the hurt is generally resolved. Sometimes a little counseling may be needed to finish things up.

As long as you feel justified in holding on to unforgiveness, you will not be able to move on. Holding on to hurt is like holding onto a poisonous snake. You must open your hand to let go. You need to open your heart to let go of what ails it. To break the hold of these destructive emotions, you have to be willing to let go to move on.

## Thinking and Perception

Low-energy negative emotions are the result, as all emotions are, of your thinking. This includes your perception, how you interpret what has happened to you. We covered how thinking works in a previous chapter, but we need to look at how it applies to low-energy emotions.

A divorce can lead to depression in some people. How you think about the divorce, not what happened to you leads to depression. If a person continues to think negatively about the divorce or their ex-spouse, they will become stuck in their negative emotions.

If a person deals with the divorce in an appropriate and positive way as quickly as possible, then looks for positive ways to make adjustments in their life, they will recover quicker and move on faster than those who do not.

Disappointments in life can stop you in your tracks and keep you from moving forward in the present. Hopefully, after reading this chapter, you will decide it is time to let your disappointments and discouragements go. Many successful businessmen I have talked with have had business failures, even multiple ones. But these men never allowed how they felt about those losses and past failures from stopping them from shaking the dust off and trying it again.

There is no timeline for how long it takes to resolve grief, get over depression, or disappointment. You decide when you are going to let it go and move forward. There are no rules as to how long these emotions should affect your life. The only rules are the ones you have made up and tell yourself.

The reason some people tend to bounce back much quicker from low-energy emotions is that they do not put roadblocks in their path like holding on to past grievances. They make choices to address what they are feeling, deal with their problems, work on repairing relationships and look for different ways to improve their lives.

A problem with low-energy emotions is personalizing what happens to you. Let me clarify what I mean by this. A person you are in a relationship with says something that hurts your feelings. Was what the person said to you something personal? Yes, but that does not mean you have to take it in a personal way? This may sound crazy, but hold on.

A person was sharing with me about her adolescent children and some of the hurtful things they would say when they did not get what they wanted. Her children were aware of how this affected their mother. Was what they were saying personal? Certainly, based on their relationship. Something a stranger says to us should not be taken personally, but we do.

She had two choices she could make when this happened. Option one is to take what they said personally. This will result in her feeling hurt and then arguing with her kids about their lack of respect. Option two. Deal with her emotions first, and then address the issue with her children afterward. Learning not to take everything personally in life is difficult, but it frees you up. When you make it personal, it makes it harder to resolve.

The problem in these types of situations is that when you take it personally, you get stuck on how you feel. When this becomes your focus, it does not help you resolve the issue that caused you to feel hurt. Many of the low-energy emotions are the result of being hurt by others. These things are personal, but you need to get your focus off taking them personally. If you can learn how to get past the hurt and focus on the real problem, you can decide how to address the problem.

Low-energy emotions lead to a *"woe is me"* syndrome. This mode of thinking is focused on ourselves, why does this happen to me.

You have to get over it. It happens to everyone. Once you get out of the "me" mindset, you will be able to see things clearer and be able to focus on overcoming these troubling emotions.

## Taking Control Over Low-Energy Emotions

The first thing you will need to do with low-energy emotions is to fight the tendency to give in to what you feel. The second thing is how you are thinking.

Alert. You will need to do the opposite of how you feel and think. If your brain is telling you to stay in bed, then you need to get out of bed. If it is telling you to not eat, then you need to eat. If it is telling you that you do not want to be around people, then you call a friend and go out for lunch. If it is telling you to give up or quit something you wanted to accomplish, then it is time to make the extra effort to fight the tendency to give in to the emotion. If it is telling you not to forgive, then forgive.

You may have to force yourself to make these decisions and exert the energy you need to fight how you feel. It is important you understand that the longer the low-energy emotion is allowed to play out in your life, draining your energy, the more entrenched the emotion becomes.

When I was a student at UNLV my mother experienced a bout of clinical depression. She stayed in bed for days at a time, had no energy, was isolating herself, and not eating.

I began to work with her by getting her out of bed each day, making her clean up and get dressed, get out of the house, socialize, and eat. Depression can affect a person's ability to perform these basic daily tasks of life. I had to force her to do things her brain was saying no to. I was acting like an external brain trying to jump-start her battery.

This became our regular routine day after day until the depression lifted, which took about two to three weeks. She gradually began to feel herself again and started doing things for herself. Everything I had my mother do was the opposite of what she wanted to do.

This is a major problem with depression, giving in to how you feel, instead of fighting it. You must fight against the urge to give in to the negative thinking that comes with depression and other low-energy emotions. Low-energy emotions are destructive.

It is important you do things that stimulate the brain's natural production of serotonin, dopamine, and norepinephrine. When the neurotransmitters are functioning properly, they result in good brain health. There are things that have been suggested in this book that can help you to stimulate your brain in positive ways that encourage brain health such as, physical activity, nutritious eating, positive hobbies, and socializing with good friends.

Good brain health can also come through acknowledging past mistakes, recognizing past accomplishments, forgiving others, laughing more and having fun, expressing thankfulness and gratitude for your life, family, and all of your blessings.

I have seen adults in counseling who have held onto their negative emotions for years, unwilling to let them go. The usual reason for this is due to a grievance they have against another person who they feel needs to pay a price for what they did. If you think like this, you will forever be stuck in your self-made misery. Be objective about what you are feeling. Focus on what you need to do for yourself. Make the changes you need to make.

Get outside of yourself regularly by thinking about others. Do not get stuck inside yourself by thinking only about yourself. Find someone who needs help and then help them, and then keep doing it. Helping people is a very powerful way to break the hold of these low-energy emotions, especially depression. Why? Because these low-energy emotions turn you inward. When you focus outward by helping someone else, there is a powerful release of neurotransmitters in your brain. Think about the young man who returned the iPhone and the positive emotions he felt by thinking about another person.

Every kid in my Corrective Thinking classes who made a legitimate attempt to help someone else reported having a positive feeling after doing this. The interesting thing was that the bigger the act of kindness, like returning a wallet with money in it someone had dropped, compared to opening a door for an elderly person, the greater the act of kindness the stronger the positive feelings. Do not underestimate the power of getting outside of yourself by doing acts of kindness to overcome low-energy negative emotions.

It has been said that to give is better than receive. That seems hard to believe in a time where we have become very self-centered as a society. King Solomon said long ago, "There is one who scatters, yet increases more; And there is one who withholds more than is right, but it leads to poverty." (Proverbs 11:24-25.)

Giving to others enriches your life. Reaching out to others helps to break your internalized negative focus. In addition, anything you do to help others will be returned to you, sometimes even more so than what you give or do. When you withhold from others, you dry up inside. Giving to others opens up the waters of life within you.

Dr. Karl Menninger, a famous doctor and founder of the Menninger Clinic was asked, "If you knew a person was heading for a nervous breakdown what would you suggest?" Everyone expected that the famous psychiatrist would say, make an appointment with a psychiatrist as soon as possible, but he didn't. Instead, he said, "Lock your door, go across the railroad tracks, and help someone in need!"

Although these low-energy negative emotions turn you inward, are deadly and destructive, you have the power to overcome them. Reaching out to others is one of the best ways to do this. Start today by finding someone you can help.

# Stress 101: The Basics

*"Reality is the leading cause of stress
among those in touch with it."*
-Lily Tomlin

Although I do not have the time to address all of the negative emotions independently, I want to focus on one specific emotion, stress. This chapter is a Stress 101 class approach, the basics. I will focus on what you need to know to learn how to control stress. I chose stress because it is the most common emotion people experience. Emotions like stress complicate life and make things difficult for us.

## Stress: Defined

Stress is defined as a state of mental tension or worry that produces negative energy. Stress results in a physiological response felt as mental tension and negative energy. Stress always generates a mental, emotional, and physical response in your body.

Stress can result from a challenge, demand, or adversity that you need to overcome, or a problem you need to resolve. Stress can be created when a person does not believe they have the ability to meet the challenge or demand, overcome the adversity, or solve the problem.

I want to emphasize this point.

- A challenge or demand is something that needs to be accomplished.
- Adversity is something that needs to be overcome.
- A problem is something that needs to be solved.

How you think about each one of these things can lead to stress!

Life is filled with daily challenges and demands. These challenges include time constraints, pressure to perform, illness, relationship problems, financial difficulties, and the list goes on. If a person believes they have the resources and ability to tackle and resolve these problems, they will not feel stress. It is only when a person does not believe they have the ability to do these things that they begin to feel the stress. So again, the emotion of stress is formed by your thinking or belief, not the problem itself.

## Three Types of Stress

The first type of stress is called acute stress. This is the stress we are most familiar with. You experience acute stress immediately when something happens to you in the present. The problem that led to feeling the stress is clearly in front of you and demands your attention. To relieve the stress, you need to resolve the issue that created the stress.

The acute stress response can turn on for something as simple as not being able to find your car keys. The lost keys may be followed by a thought, "You are going to be late for work." You become more anxious and grow more stressed the longer you have to look for your keys. The stress that comes with a challenge, adversity, or problem—big or small—is the result of how you think about it.

In life, there are many crises that come with losing your job to losing your keys—from not having the money to pay your bills to being late for work, all of which can lead to stress. These types of mini-crises happen regularly in life. The good news is that acute stress typically goes away when the problem is solved. But if it is not solved, it can turn into chronic stress.

Chronic stress means prolonged, ongoing stress. Chronic stress results when a problem continues for an extended period of time. These can include things like ongoing financial or health problems. Many of the probation officers I worked with felt an ongoing low level of stress. As the problem continues, so does the stress.

When you feel stressed out, you are more likely to experience other negative emotions as well. You become more sensitive to what is going on around you. Stress can cause you to react quicker emotionally, especially with anger. For many people, chronic stress becomes the problem emotion they have difficulty controlling.

Chronic stress tends to lead to ruminations, ongoing negative thinking about yourself and the situation you are dealing with. These ruminations fuel stress. This is why it is so important that you learn how to change your thinking to control your stress. Chronic stress can result from an ongoing debilitating disease. When life feels like a pressure cooker where people are surviving and not really living, mental health issues can develop like depression.

The third type of stress is cumulative stress. Cumulative stress is a combination of daily stressors and ongoing chronic stressors. This can easily be seen during stressful periods of time when job stress overlaps with the normal stressors in life.

## Psychological and Social Stress

There are two categories of stress. The first is called psychological stress. You have been learning about psychological stress, which is stress created by how you think. The second is social stress.

Social stress is based on status within a social context. Social context means where you fit in within a group of people. The context comes with a pecking order or hierarchy. Social stress is based on a person's position within a group.

People on the low rung of a pecking order are more vulnerable to social stress. This includes living at a lower socioeconomic status, including poverty. Social stress can be seen in the homeless person who has to scrap every day just to survive. People who are entering into retirement can find themselves experiencing social stress based on their previous level of income being drastically cut.

The lower a person's position is at work can create social stress. The lower you are on the work ladder, the more stress you may feel than those above you. How a person chooses to think about their status at work or life can increase or lessen the level of stress they will feel.

People who live within a lower socio-economic level are more likely to have physical and mental health problems as a result. People who are the worker bees tend to experience more work-related stress leading to health issues and taking off more sick days than those above them.

People who live in low-income areas of town where there is high poverty and high crime rates, will have more physical health issues and live a shorter life span than a person living in a gated community.

How a person chooses to handle social stress determines the level of stress they will feel. Many people who live on the lower end of the pecking order, whether in life or at work, have learned how to live in a state of contentment above the stress.

Although you may be at a lower socio-economic status in life, it does not mean that you are stuck there. You have the power to make many choices and changes about how you want to live. Feeling that you have no choices in life leads to stress due to a loss of hope.

## Only Three Things You Can Do with Stress

There are only three approaches you can take when it comes to dealing with stress.

- The first is to keep reacting like you always do. Reacting to stress changes nothing. Say that aloud to yourself. Reacting to stress changes nothing. You simply keep repeating the same old things you have done in the past leading to the same old results.
- The second thing is acceptance. Acceptance means you quit fighting the situation or person you cannot control. What is interesting here is that the acceptance of a problem you cannot change actually reduces the level of stress you feel. For instance, if you cannot change the situation with your boss, you accept this as a fact of life and learn how to live with the situation.

When you accept there is a situation or person you cannot change, your focus shifts to developing strategies of how to live with the problem or person as a part of life.

- The third is to resolve what created the stress. Resolving stress focuses on finding healthy and positive ways to solve the problem. Once you shut down the stress response, you are immediately in a position to find a solution to your problem.

## Two Important Questions to Ask

The secret behind controlling stress revolves around two important questions to ask. The first question has to do with control.

> *"Do you have the ability to control what is happening to you, or can you control what another person does?"*

If the answer to either question is no, then how does feeling stress help you change anything?

If you do not have the ability to control the situation or another person, then you need to go straight to acceptance as the solution for dealing with your stress. Quit fighting against what you cannot control. The control question can help you decide rather quickly whether your time thinking should be spent on finding a solution to the problem or developing a strategy for how to live with the situation. One of the toughest things for people to do is to let go of trying to control everything in their life. Outside of yourself, you have very little ability to control anything else.

Stress results from a loss of predictability. The second question to ask is,

> *"Can you predict with accuracy what will happen in the future?"*

The lack of predictability about the future leads to feeling stress and anxiety. Think of waiting for the lab results that will determine whether you have an illness. It is hard for most people to calmly wait for those results.

When predictability is removed in life, people begin to imagine things that could happen. Usually, what a person imagines is far worse than what actually does happen in most instances in the end. Have you ever thought something was going to happen that did not?

> *"Man is not worried by real problems, as much as by his imagined anxieties about real problems."*
> -Epictetus

Stress and anxiety come with imagining what you think will happen. Quit imagining what will happen. Quit the endless self-talk and fortune-telling about what you think will or will not happen. It has no effect on the outcome. What it does is intensify your feelings of stress and anxiety.

If you cannot predict the outcome, then accept the reality you are not able to. If you want to learn to control your stress, quit imagining what will happen. Has predicting the future outcome ever changed the outcome of what has happened in your life?

In a difficult situation whatever will happen, will happen. You have no control over it. Stressing over it before it comes makes no sense. I dare you to find one instance where feeling stressed ever made a situation better.

## Stress and a Broken Car

When was the last time your car broke down on the side of the road? What was the immediate emotional reaction you had? Maybe stress. Added to this are the many other problems that come with a breakdown, like waiting for help, finding transportation to work the next day, and the repair costs. This happened to me recently.

I was turning left on my way home when the power of my car quickly faded. I barely made the left turn with oncoming traffic ahead. I was stranded less than a mile from my home. Initially, I felt the pangs of frustration and stress.

Quickly I worked on a solution to the problem, calling my youngest son to see if he could help. As I waited for him, I had a chance to practice what I preach and do some breathing.

I realized I was not in control of what just happened. The problem was right there in front of me. My car was not going anywhere, and I could do nothing about it other than hope my son could get me home. I could choose to stress on the problem or focus on controlling the stress response. I chose to accept my situation.

Having done this, I peacefully waited for my son to arrive which took about thirty minutes. He pushed my car into the driveway where it sat till the next morning.

When I walked into the house that night, I said aloud to myself "there is nothing I can, or even want to do tonight. It can be taken care of in the morning." In essence, I was telling my brain no more thinking about it tonight.

I did not think about the car for the rest of the evening or the financial expense of fixing it. I had a great night's sleep. When I awoke the next day, I went into problem-solving mode stress-free. A few phone calls and the problem was quickly on the way to being solved without stress.

> "The greatest weapon against stress is our
> ability to choose one thought over another."
> -William James

The initial physiological response to stress was there. I felt it as soon as my car broke down. I did not have to think about feeling stress. I had a choice to make, what was I going to do about the stress? To reject the stress, I had to accept the circumstances of my broken car and focus on solving the problem. I had to reject any negative self-talk and focus on the positive. Choosing to feel or reject stress is a choice you have to make when the stress comes.

## Summary

As you put into practice the things you have learned, you will find that you have the ability to control your emotions, including stress.

- Controlling stress begins with controlling the immediate stress response by using yoga breathing to slow your heart rate down so you can think.

- Ask yourself if you have control over what is happening, or if you can predict what will happen. If the answer is no to either question, you need to give up trying to control the situation or predicting what will happen.
- Choose to accept what you cannot control. Then develop a strategy of how you will solve or live with the problem in a positive way.
- If there is a problem you can solve, then come up with a solution by using the strategies for change that you learned in an earlier chapter.
- Remember that stress is a physiological reaction to a situation based on how you think about it. You can control it; you can change it.

# 20

# *Tips for Improving Your Life*

*"If you deliberately plan on being less than
you are capable of being, then I warn you that
you'll be unhappy for the rest of your life."*
-Abraham H. Maslow

I offer a similar thought that goes like this, "If you do not work on being the best you can be, you will always settle for being second best, or less."

To be less than your full potential in life, all you have to do is give up and quit trying. Simply quit working at improving yourself. Sit back passively and let whatever is going to happen, happen. No one has to make an effort to stay the same or fail. It comes naturally. I guarantee you the longer you coast through life, the less satisfying your life will become.

When a person believes in themselves and starts to take control of their life, everything in life can change. I want to close out with some tips for change. These are simple and practical truths that you can use each day to improve your life.

*Brad Garrett*

# Things You Need to Change

> *"You cannot have a positive life and a negative mind."*
> -Joyce Meyer

## Stop Focusing on the Negatives: A Positive Viewpoint Lifts You Up.

Every day you have choices to make. One of those choices is whether you are going to focus on the negative or the positive of what is going on around you.

A negative viewpoint influences your thinking and behavior. It affects your emotions in negative ways. If you get dust in your eye, it will distort your ability to see clearly. In the same way, when you look at life from a negative point of view, it distorts how you see things. It will hinder your ability to see the positive in life and opportunities for success.

You do not have to look hard to find the negative, the negatives will always be there. If you are a person who gravitates to the negative it will take an extra effort to break this tendency. Choices come in life with at least two options, do this or do that. You cannot do both. You choose each day whether you will focus on the positive or negative things of life. No one makes that choice for you.

I have met people who have become so negatively focused they talk themselves out of doing things they could easily do. I have seen people turn down a job because it did not fit into their desired schedule. How does getting a job that pays money to provide for food and pay the bills become a negative in life? A negative focus will keep you stuck where you are at.

About five to six years ago, I became aware of how negative the news had become and the negative effect it was having on me. Once I became aware of this I said, "No thanks," and canceled my subscription to the local newspaper, and turned off the nightly news. Immediately, the agitation I had been feeling created by these programs was gone.

When you understand the negative effect something has on you, then there is a choice you can make. You have the power to choose what you listen to and watch. Turning off the negative influences in your life, including people, is a great choice for improving your emotional health.

*"If you could only change one thing in your life, I believe that choosing to focus on being positive every day will make the greatest impact in your life."*

## Stop the Negative Thinking: Positive Thinking Feels Better

Stop thinking about the negative side of everything. You need to turn the coin over and look on the positive side. Stop thinking about what you cannot do, or the reasons it will fail to happen if you try to do it. Start believing in what you can do.

Negative thinking is influenced by the things you choose to spend your time watching, reading, and listening to. You need to become aware of how things and people around you influence your thinking.

Negative thinking is a choice. It is like pouring a little poison into a glass of water. All of the water becomes poisoned. Negative thinking poisons your thinking and the choices you make. It is hurtful in your relationships. Negative thinking is common for many people.

Try this exercise. Go through a 24-hour day and every time you become aware of negative thinking, stop it and then take the time to turn it into a positive thought. After you do this, write down the negative thinking you had and how you were able to change it to a positive thought. This will heighten your awareness of how often during the day your thinking is focused on the negative and how to change it.

## Get Rid of Your Bad Attitude

Getting rid of a bad attitude changes you first, then the situation. A bad attitude came with many of the teenagers I worked with who were on probation. Do you know anyone who has a bad attitude? Are they fun to be around?

A bad attitude can manifest with "I know it all," or with "no one can tell me what to do." Two other bad attitudes are "I am entitled," and "I am special." Bad attitudes can be seen in people who are grumpy, irritable, or are angry.

Negative attitudes are behind the rudeness and insensitivity to others you see today. Entitlement thinking has become a plague in today's culture. You can see the "I am entitled" thinking manifested in the number of young adults who live at home with their parents, not working, but expecting their parents to continue to meet their needs.

A bad attitude can keep a person from hearing what others are saying to them, even when that person is trying to help them. A bad attitude will drive people away from you. To make healthy progress in life you must rid yourself of any negative focus, thinking, or attitudes you have. Positive is the way to go.

## Stop Complaining: Do Something About It

Have you ever noticed that some people are complainers? They always seem to find something to complain about, but they do not have solutions. Complainers focus on the negative of everything, and usually never do anything to change things to make it better. How does complaining help make things better?

I am not saying that at times there are not some legitimate complaints. However, complaining will not accomplish what needs to happen in your life. People complain about their spouses, their children, their jobs, their health, and how difficult it is to get ahead. Complaining changes this?

It is the doers in life who change the things others are complaining about. When the complaint is legitimate, like bad customer service, you can speak to the manager, or choose not to go back to the restaurant. Think for a minute how you felt when you registered that complaint. Complaining does not generate positive feelings. Stop it!

## Stop Arguing with People

Arguing begins small and grows in the heat of anger. The problem with arguing is that a lot of people seem to enjoy arguing. They would not admit to that, but why else would they continually do it? If they are not enjoying it then it simply has become a bad habit.

Stop arguing and learn to discuss differences and work out disagreements. Learn to find common ground. Working up your emotions by arguing is not a good thing. Arguing generally revolves around who is right and who wins. This is not an emotionally healthy way to approach communication in a relationship. Communication should always be geared toward a solution. Becoming a better listener will go a long way in improving your communication in relationships.

> "It is honorable for a man to stop striving,
> since any fool can start a quarrel."
> Proverb 20:3

## Stop Blaming People or Circumstances

If you want to take control of your life, you will have to stop blaming others for your problems, how you feel, where you are at in life, and any lack of progress. You cannot blame circumstances either. Difficult people and difficult circumstances are a part of life. You need to learn how to be an overcomer, not a victim. If all you can do is blame circumstances or others for not making progress, you are stuck.

Blaming others for how you feel or for your problems takes away your power to overcome them. Blame seems so natural. It has to be what someone said, or they did, that caused me to feel this way. It is their fault, not mine. This can be the first thought when things start to go south.

When you look for someone or something to fix the blame on, you lose sight of fixing the problem. Once you stop playing the blame game, the focus shifts back on to you to solve the problem; what are you going to do about it?

> "Fix the problem, not the blame."
> -Sean Connery from Rising Sun

## Quit Recalling Past Hurts, Disappointments, and Failures

To stop living in the past is hard to do when you have been victimized and hurt. I have witnessed the difference between people who have become stuck in their life because of past hurts, versus those that have resolved them and moved on in life. Holding on to past hurts by continually bringing them up stops you from growing.

Once you rid yourself of the past and the hold it has on you, your life will improve dramatically, and your future will look brighter too. Holding on to the past is like wearing shackles around your feet. You can still get around, but not as far or as quick as you can when you remove the shackles. Once you unshackle yourself from the past, you will find you are free to take your life whichever direction you want it to go.

Whatever happened to you was probably unfair and should never have happened to you. Do not let the past take away your power to change. You must make a decision about what you will do with your past going forward. You have a choice; what will you choose to do?

Some of you may need a professional counselor to help you work through your past trauma.

## Stop Fortune-Telling

The thing about fortune telling is that people usually predict the worse outcomes will happen. Usually, they do not. Fortune telling creates a lot of stress and anxiety.

Thinking about something that might not happen is wasted energy. Living in the present means focusing on the moment. Try listening to as many conversations taking place around you as you can over the next week. Include with this what you hear on news programs. How much time was spent predicting what may happen in those conversations?

When was the last time you predicted an outcome you thought was going to happen that did not? Think of all the wasted mental energy and negative emotions you felt spending time thinking about what you thought was going to happen.

When you realize you are the one creating your anxiety or stress by predicting what you think will happen, it makes no sense to continue to do this. Even if something bad could happen like losing a job, you have a choice of how you are going to deal with it if and when it happens. Worrying about losing your job before it happens does not do one thing to stop it from happening. Learn to patiently wait for the outcome.

## Learn to Flip Your Switch

Remember that emotion is the energy you feel in your body. Flipping the switch is what you do to turn a light on or off. Learn to flip the switch when you want to shut down an emotional reaction or bad behavior. You need to flip the switch of negative thinking and bad attitudes too.

## Train Yourself to Look for the Positives

Although we have talked about this, it needs to be reiterated. If you have been a person who has spent more time looking at the negatives in life than the positives, it will take an extra effort to transition to looking for the positives in life. As you do this, your effort will be rewarded.

Winners do not give up, do not quit, and do not throw in the towel. Winners focus on today, what they need to do, and look for the positive that makes things happen.

## Look for Opportunities to Help Others

One of the fastest changes I saw probation kids make was the week they had to do one act of random kindness for a stranger. Now, this may have only been a temporary change, but I do not know that. What these teenagers experienced was what it feels like to take the focus off themselves for a minute and focus on doing something for someone else.

Doing something kind for someone creates positive emotions. This is the brain's way of rewarding us. When you do something good for someone, the brain responds by saying "I'm going to give you a good feeling," and positive emotions result. Every time I personally give money to someone standing at a traffic light or on a street corner, I know I am doing the right thing and a positive feeling is generated.

This is similar to the law of reaping and sowing. If you sow good deeds, you will be rewarded, at the very least with positive emotions. Have you ever done something for another person and then in the next week or month when you need help someone is there for you? On the other hand, have you ever turned someone down that you could have given a dollar to? How did you feel afterward?

## Level of Effort Determines Level of Success

Your level of effort determines your level of success. What you get out of something is proportionally equal to what you put into it. The greater the effort, the greater the outcome.

I want to use this principle with money and a savings account. If you put ten dollars a week in the bank for a year, at the end of the year you could withdraw five hundred and twenty dollars out of the bank. If you deposited one hundred dollars a week for a year, you could withdraw five thousand, two hundred and fifty dollars at the end of the year.

To save one hundred dollars a week will require you to make a greater effort and bigger sacrifice than ten dollars a week. But the end result is ten times greater based on the extra effort.

This principle is true regarding the amount of change you will make in your life at any given time. The more effort and energy you put into bringing about the change, the quicker the change occurs.

Give it all you got, and the rest will take care of itself.

## Practice Makes Perfect

I was seven years old and did not know how to hit or throw a baseball very well, but baseball looked like fun. I became a batboy for some kids I knew who were three years older than myself. One day the team had only eight kids for the game. They did not want to forfeit so they recruited me to play that day. They felt the safest place to put me was in the right field. There were very few left-handed hitters back then.

Beginning at the age of seven, I played baseball all the way through high school. With practice, I became good enough to play on the varsity baseball team as a sophomore. What happened between the ages of seven to seventeen-years-old? Practice, and lots of it.

The things you have been learning throughout the book you will need to practice over and over until you become proficient and it becomes the way you live. Practice makes perfect.

# What Have You Learned?

## Slow Down, Calm Down, Now Think

*Breathing* slows your heart rate, slowing down the adrenaline. This helps you calm down and refocus. You stop reacting to what is happening. Breathing lessens the tension in your body helping you to feel more relaxed. Practice yoga breathing until it becomes the way you breathe.

*Timeout* means you stop what you are doing right now. You walk away from the situation or the person that triggered the emotional reaction. After you have had time to calm down and regain your focus, you can then decide if you need to return to address the issue with the other person. If not, move on. Sometimes when you calm down you find that it is not that important and let it go.

*Redirect the energy* created by the emotion. Instead of doing what you have done in the past when you get angry or feel stressed, redirect the energy into something positive like exercising, riding a bike, jogging, or going for a walk.

*Stop technique* is a simple technique that works in stopping repetitive thoughts and rumination. When you have a thought you do not want to have, or if you catch yourself starting to do a behavior you want to change, you say "stop it" to yourself, even out loud. Then you keep saying it until the thought is gone.

When I would teach this technique to a group of adolescents, I would purposely speak in a monotone voice and then yell, "Stop it!" Some kids would jump, while others would say something. But I had everyone's eyes on me.

I would explain that when I said "stop it," whatever they were thinking at that moment was gone and the focus was on me. It broke their train of thought, which is the purpose of this technique. The stop technique is especially helpful with negative self-talk. It is a simple thing to learn to do, which works by interrupting the negative thinking, allowing you time to refocus.

Remember, slow down, calm down, and take the time to think.

## Emotional Balance

*Maintain your emotional balance* is a goal that should be pursued every day.

*Prayer and faith* are two of the most powerful things that you can do for good emotional, mental, and spiritual health. Prayer and faith give people hope! Even people who do not have any type of religious background or do not go to church, find comfort in prayer in times of crisis. Faith is a powerful tool to help you make changes in your life.

*Meditation* stimulates the brain in a positive way. It can help bring about an inner state of peacefulness. *Massage* helps to relieve the tightness in your muscles that comes with stress and negative emotions. *Yoga and Tai Chi* are great for relaxation.

*Stress relief hobbies* should be activities that are fun, healthy, and stimulate the brain. I do not count sitting at your desk at home surfing the Internet as a hobby. I personally have an area in my house for working on puzzles. At the end of the day, while working on a one-thousand-piece puzzle, I let everything go and relax. When you focus on a hobby you enjoy, nothing else matters, and relaxation follows.

*When you leave work, leave work.* It is not just the physical work some people bring home with them, it is the emotional stress and turmoil created at work. To maintain your emotional balance, you must make your home a safe place, a place for enjoyment and relaxation. If you were working in your yard and stepped into a mud puddle, would you keep your shoe on when you went into your home? I hope not! In the same way, you pollute your home when you bring all the negative things that happen each day at work home with you. Stop It.

*Eat right.* The importance of eating right plays an important role in having a good brain and physical health. A healthy diet is important for good mental and emotional health too. A healthy diet can go a long way in reshaping a new you.

*Sleep tight.* Sleeping right equates to between seven to nine hours a night for an adult. This means restful sleep, apart from a bathroom break. I hear some people say, "I only need 5 to 6 hours." That may be true, but inadequate sleep over time will catch up with you sooner or later.

Sleep is important for good mental and emotional health. During sleep, your brain renews itself, eliminates brain toxins, and helps to repair the body. Things you spent time learning are filed away to be used at a later date or discarded altogether.

A lack of sleep, or too much sleep, can be a symptom of a developing mental health problem. If you sleep less than what is recommended and have good brain health, then stay your course. But do the research for yourself on how important sleep is. With a good night's sleep, you awaken refreshed and ready for the new day.

## Be Aware and Identify

*Awareness* is where change begins.

*Identify the stimulus* that created the emotion.

*Identify the emotion* you feel. Remember there can be a second emotion underneath the one you feel. You can feel angry at someone, but the anger can cover over the hurt you feel by what they said or did.

*Identify your thinking* and how it contributed to how you feel. It is not the problem that creates the emotion, it is how you think about the problem.

*Identify any ruminating thoughts or negative self-talk.* Stop it!

*Identify the immediate behavior* that comes with an emotional response, as well as any problem behaviors you repeatedly struggle with, and change how you think about them.

## Change

*Focus on permanent change, not a temporary change.* The temporary change would be similar to going on a diet to fit into a bathing suit. When beach season is over you go back to your old behavior and gain the weight back. Permanent change is lasting change. It becomes a part of the way you live. Superficial change only lasts for so long. Permanent change changes your life.

*Replace the old way of thinking.* As you have learned you will have to develop a new way of thinking. When you truly change how you think, you will change how you feel, and behavior change will follow.

## Reinforce Lifestyle Changes

*Apply what you learn.* If all you do is read this book, then your life will probably not change. Getting new knowledge is good, but knowledge needs to be applied for it to become meaningful.

*Practice what you have learned.* With anything in life, a person gets better with practice. You will have some hits and misses when you are starting out, but as you practice you will become more proficient. You will find you are struggling less to control your emotions and change bad behavior. Regular practice speeds up the learning curve.

> "We are what we repeatedly do. Excellence
> then is not an act, but a habit."
> -Aristotle

*Maintain a desire to be a better person.* At some point in life, it can be easier to settle into the backseat than it is to take the driver's seat to improve your life. You are never too old to change Life is never too difficult to make changes. No one can give you the desire to want to improve your life or be successful. You must do this for yourself.

*Expand your knowledge base. Educate yourself.* I have noticed some adults think they have learned everything in life, teenagers too. This results in no longer spending time reading and learning new things. Reading this book has hopefully taught you some new things that you can apply to your life to make changes. Keep it going by reading some of the books I have recommended.

My mother was a Licensed Practical Nurse who taught me that no matter what a doctor might tell me, go check it out for myself. Her purpose in doing this was to teach me to educate myself. This was great advice and has led to learning many things that I might have missed if I had not followed her advice. There is far more to life that we do not know about, and far more than we will ever be able to learn. You can learn how to improve your life, reach your full potential, and live a life filled with joy and peace.

> "When you're through learning, you're through."
> -Will Rogers

# Conclusion

Let's return to Maple Street, USA.

The people in the story were portrayed as average citizens like you and me. The story portrays, with a level of accuracy, what happens when people's emotions take over, their thinking becomes irrational based on faulty information, and how the aggressive and violent can follow.

What did you see in 2020?

Instead of the big picture of what has happened and has been carried over to 2021, I am focusing on the smaller picture, you. Why?

Once the people became a mob, behaving as one under group think, individual thought was lost. I can speak to you, but not a mob. How are you at controlling the monster now that you understand what it means? This book was written to let you know he can be defeated.

## Last Thoughts

- Appreciate the value of stress, anger, and anxiety reduction in your life.
- Change your bad habits into new and productive ones.
- Learn to forgive and let go.
- Reach out and help others. To give is better than to receive.
- Develop an attitude of gratitude. Thankfulness is one of the most powerful ways to put your life into the proper perspective.
- Share what you have learned in this book with others to help them on their life's journey.

# NOTES

1. W. Doyle Gentry, *Anger Management for Dummies*, Wiley Publishing Inc., Hoboken, New Jersey, 2007.
2. Mark Hyman, *The Blood Sugar Solution*, New York, N.Y., Little Brown and Company. 2012, pg. Dedication.
3. *Commitment to Change, Volume One, Part Two, Two Crucial Mistakes*, FMS Productions, Stanton Samenow presenter.
4. Ibid
5. *Commitment to Change, Volume One, Part Two, Two Crucial Mistakes*, FMS Productions, Stanton Samenow presenter.